# THE YOUNG ATHLETE'S MANUAL

**OTHER BOOKS BY ROBERT GARDNER**

Kitchen Chemistry

Save That Energy

Water: The Life Sustaining Resource

The Whale Watchers' Guide

# THE YOUNG ATHLETE'S MANUAL

ROBERT GARDNER

Drawings by Frank Cecala

**JULIAN MESSNER**
NEW YORK

Text copyright © 1985 by Robert Gardner
Drawings copyright © 1985 by Frank Cecala

Published by Julian Messner,
A Division of Simon & Schuster, Inc.
Simon & Schuster Building
Rockefeller Center
1230 Avenue of the Americas
New York, New York 10020

JULIAN MESSNER and colophon are
trademarks of Simon & Schuster, Inc.

Manufactured in the United States of America

Library of Congress Cataloguing in Publication Data

Gardner, Robert, 1929–
    The young athlete's manual.

    Bibliography: p.
    Includes index.
    Summary: Discusses the exercises, diet, and mental
attitude needed to acquire strength and fitness and to
train for such sports as basketball, baseball, hockey,
and others.
    1. Physical education and training—Juvenile literature.
2. Physical fitness—Juvenile literature. [1. Physical
education and training. 2. Physical fitness] I. Title.
GV711.5.G37  1985      613.7′1      85-8864
ISBN: 0-671-49369-8

10  9  8  7  6  5  4  3

# Acknowledgments

My thanks to Bruce Blodgett, Russ Edes, John Gardner, Morgan Schafer, and Dennis Shortelle for their helpful suggestions and comments. All are competent coaches with whom I have been associated in one way or another for a number of years.

Again, to my wife Natalie, my sincere thanks for typing yet another manuscript.

# Contents

*If all the year were playing holidays,*
*To sport would be as tedious as to*
*work.*

# So You Want to Be an Athlete

You throw the ball into the air. As your racquet reaches the apex of its path above your outstretched arm, it meets the ball squarely, flattening one side of the sphere. A powerful follow-through sends the ball into your opponent's court just inside the center line. So fast does the ball move that your opponent is frozen in place. You have won the deciding set.

The cheering crowd rises. As you round first base, you can see the ball high above the center field fence. You have hit a game-winning homer in the final game of the playoffs.

The ball appears to hang motionless at the edge of the cup before it falls into the eighteenth hole, giving you a birdie and the best score in the state tournament.

You feel as though your lungs will burst, and the sounds of your opponents' feet striking the cinder-covered track seem to be growing louder. With a final surge of speed, made possible by energy you didn't think you possessed, you break away from the pack and cross the finish line with a time that sets a school record.

The swish of the ball through the net accompanies the bzzzz of the game-ending buzzer and the roar of the fans. Your jump shot from the corner has broken the tie and given your team the state championship.

These are dreams of young athletes, dreams that sometimes become realities, dreams that often are shattered by disappointment. In either case, the fun of playing, the challenges you face, and the benefits that exercise has for your body make the pursuit of your favorite sport worthwhile.

Most young athletes come to realize, at some point in their teenage years, that they are not cut out to compete at the professional or perhaps even at the college or high school level. After all, relatively few people play professional or college sports. So be prepared for disappointment if you want to be a professional athlete. Develop alternate career plans in case your dream does not come true. On the other hand, you may be among the few who succeed in the competition for places in high school, college, Olympic, or professional sports. Even if you decide not to enter such competition, you can still be one of the vast majority who find athletics an enjoyable, relaxing, and rewarding form of recreation.

Competition, determination, cooperation through

teamwork, the thrill of winning, and the ability to lose gracefully and with dignity—all of these important benefits of athletics will be of value throughout your life.

For some of you, athletics will provide a lifelong vocation. For those few of you who become professional athletes, play will become your work for at least a short segment of your life. For others, coaching, physical education, sportswriting, sports broadcasting, sales, management, advertising, officiating, even law, medicine, or psychology may provide a sports-related career. But all of us should realize that athletics, which serve a valuable and healthful role in our lives, are not the be-all and end-all of life.

If formal team sports were eliminated from our nation's colleges and universities, we could still exercise and participate in informal sports. But if these same institutions closed their medical and dental schools and their other graduate and undergraduate programs, people's well-being would be at stake. Our society—which is based on our citizens' learned skills, attitudes, and comprehension of the world's complexities—could not survive without our institutions of learning.

Whether or not you seek to become a professional athlete, your primary goal should be to obtain a good education. An education will provide you with greater salary potential. But more important than money is the quality of life that learning provides. It opens new avenues of awareness, insights, interests, and enjoyment while providing a richer, more encompassing view of society, history, culture, science, and our universe—a world that those who leave school too soon will never know unless they educate themselves.

For the student athlete, time is a precious commodity. To use your time most efficiently, make a chart of the hours for each day of the week. Block out time for sleep, classes, games, practice sessions, meals, and other required activities. You can use the remaining hours for study or recreation. Decide how you want to use those hours. Write in the amount of time you need to study each subject. You can do lengthy assignments such as papers or test preparations on Sundays so that you don't have to stay up late during the week. If you have difficulty studying efficiently, consult a fellow student or teacher who is knowledgeable in study techniques, or read some of the many books and pamphlets available on this subject.

To follow a demanding schedule, you must be organized, disciplined, and dedicated. It requires intense concentration and a willingness to limit social events, television, and other forms of recreation. If you can make such sacrifices, maintain a positive attitude, think of yourself as a winner, cut off extraneous stimuli, and concentrate on the task at hand, you probably have the mental qualities to be a successful athlete. Such qualities give you a definite edge over competitors with equal physical ability and even over some competitors who may possess more natural ability. Any coach will tell you that confidence, fluid intelligence, patience, self-control, concentration, discipline, enthusiasm, desire to succeed, mental toughness, alertness, commitment, the ability to function well under stress, and a willingness to sacrifice for the sake of the team are at least as important as such physical qualities as strength, coordination, power, agility, balance, quickness, and speed.

In this book you will learn how to improve your

athletic potential by strengthening and stretching your muscles properly. Such exercises will not only make you stronger and more supple but will also help to prevent the injuries that plague so many athletes.

You will also learn how to train for certain specific sports, how to eat properly, how to determine what kind of physical shape you are in, and how to prevent and treat common athletic injuries. Finally, you will learn about the psychological aspects of sports—how to relax, concentrate, and avoid the psych-out.

First, you'll learn how to stretch your muscles properly. Stretching should precede any athletic activity so let's begin there.

# Stretching

Many physicians claim that 80 percent of all athletic injuries are related to poor flexibility. Our flexibility is determined by the elasticity, or suppleness, of the connective tissue that surrounds our joints. Any strenuous exercise tends to increase muscle tightness and reduce flexibility. Stretching, both before and after exercise, will keep you flexible and help prevent injuries, stiffness, discomfort, and pain associated with vigorous exercise.

Stretching should be relaxing and enjoyable. It should not be done in a competitive manner. If stretching causes pain, you are probably overstretching, which can cause injury.

Before you begin stretching your muscles, do a few warm-up exercises. Running in place, clap-straddles, and burpees are all good warm-ups. To do a clap-straddle, you clap your hands above your head as you jump and spread your feet. Then bring your hands

back to your sides as you again jump and bring your feet together. Repeat this warm-up about 20 times.

To do a burpee, move from a standing position to a forward crouch with your hands on the floor in front

of your feet. With your hands supporting your upper body, push both feet backward so that you are in a push-up position. Then bring your feet back to where they were, putting your body again in a crouch. Finally, rise to your original erect stance. Repeat this exercise 10 to 20 times.

Move slowly as you stretch muscles to the point where you feel mild tension. Hold the stretched position for 10 to 20 seconds. Don't bounce! Exhale as you enter into a stretch; then breathe naturally. Don't hold your breath while stretching. Relax. This is called the "easy stretch." By the end of 10 to 20 seconds, the mild tension should have disappeared. Now move into the "developmental stretch" by extending your muscles a very short distance until you again feel mild tension. Hold this developmental stretch for another 10 to 20 seconds.

The following stretching sequence is designed to stretch all your muscles before and after exercise. Some specific stretching techniques for certain sports or muscles will be given later.

1. **Neck muscles:** (a) With hands on hips, slowly roll your head in a full circle, keeping your back straight. If you find tight places, hold the stretch at that point. Relax and let the tightness fade. Then go on. (b) Turn your head slowly to the right as far as you can. Repeat, turning your head to the left.

2. **Shoulders:** (a) Put your right forearm behind your head. Grab your right elbow with your left hand and gently pull the elbow behind your head to the point where you feel mild tension. Lean slowly to the left. Repeat in the other direction, holding your left elbow with your right hand. (b) Slowly swing your extended arms from the sides across your chest. (c) Slowly swing your arms in full vertical circles.

3. **Waist:** With your feet apart at shoulder width, left hand on hip, and right hand extended above your head, bend slowly at the waist to your left. Hold at the first sensation of tension. Repeat, bending to the right.

4. **Hamstrings (muscles in the backs of your legs) and lower back:** From the same position in which you began Exercise 3, bend forward slowly at the hips. Keep your knees slightly bent to avoid stress on your lower back. Bend forward until you feel the first tension. You may be able to place your fingertips or even your palms on the floor, depending on your body proportions and flexibility, but don't overstretch. Let your arms hang loose. Relax. When you return slowly to an erect position, stand with your feet flat and your knees bent. This will tighten the quadriceps (the muscles in the front of your

thighs) and relax the hamstrings. Then repeat the stretch.

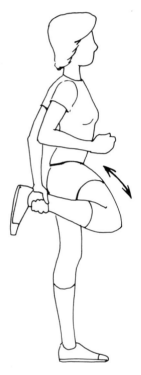

5. **Knee and thigh:** (a) Behind your back, grab your left foot with your right hand. Slowly pull the foot toward your buttocks until you feel tension; then hold the stretch. Repeat with your other leg. (b) Spread your feet about 2½ feet apart. Squat so that your elbows rest on your thighs. After 20 seconds, slowly shift your weight to the right, then to the left, while remaining in the squat position. Don't do this stretch if you have a knee injury.

6. **Groin and inner thighs:** With your feet about 3 feet apart, stretch to one side with your knee bent and shift your weight onto that knee. The other leg

should stretch until you feel slight tension in the groin area where the leg joins the body. Slowly shift your weight to your other knee and stretch your other leg. Repeat this exercise several times.

7. **Groin, hamstring, and calf:** Assume the position you would take to do a split. (But don't try to do one.) Use both hands, one on each side of your body, for balance. Keep your left leg straight with the heel on the floor and the toes pointed upward. Repeat the exercise, this time stretching your right leg.

8. **Groin:** From a sitting position, bring your feet in toward your body. Place the soles of your feet together. Hold your ankles and use your elbows to press on the insides of both knees. Press the knees downward to stretch your groin.

9. **Groin and hamstring:** Sit with your legs spread as wide as possible. Grab one ankle or lower leg with both hands and try to place your forehead on that

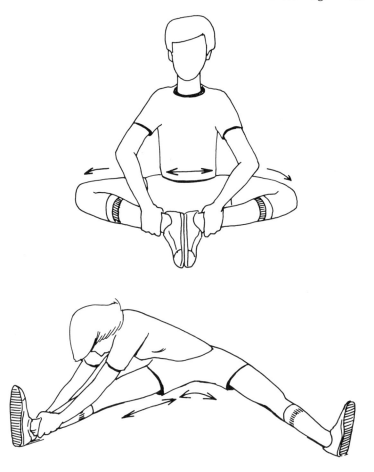

knee. Let your quadriceps muscles relax as you do
this stretch so that your hamstring can be fully
stretched. Repeat stretch on other side.

10. **Achilles tendon and back:** Sit on the floor with your
legs together. Grab your toes and slowly pull the
front halves of your feet toward your chest, stretching the Achilles tendon. Let the quadriceps relax.

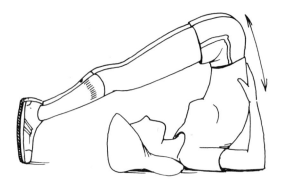

11. **Back:** From a sitting position, slowly roll back-
    ward, bringing your feet and legs over your head.
    Use your hands to support your hips and control
    the stretch. Touch your toes to the floor above your
    head. As you roll back to a sitting position, put your
    hands under your knees and roll very slowly.
12. **Body:** Stand erect with the fingers of both hands
    interlaced in front of you. Raise your arms while
    turning your palms outward. Stand on your toes
    and try to touch the ceiling with your upstretched
    palms.
    You should do these general stretches before and
    after each workout.

## SUPPLEMENTARY STRETCHING

If certain muscles of your body seem unusually tight
or have recently been injured, these additional
stretching exercises may be necessary to obtain good
flexibility.

13. **Back:** (a) Lying on your back with your knees bent,
    tighten your gluteus (butt) and abdominal muscles
    at the same time to flatten your lower back against
    the floor. Hold for 5 to 10 seconds. Relax, and then

repeat several times. This will help relieve lower back tension.

(b) From the same supine (flat-on-your-back) position, with your hands folded behind your neck, pull your shoulderblades together to create tension in your upper back. After about 5 seconds, relax and pull your head forward, moving your chin toward your chest and stretching your neck.

(c) From the same position, extend your arms above your head and straighten your legs. Stretch your arms and legs as far as you can in opposite directions. Stretch for about 5 seconds. Relax and then stretch your right leg and left arm. Then your left leg and right arm. Then stretch both arms and legs again.

(d) Again, in supine position, grab your right knee with both hands and pull it to your chest while keeping your back flat on the floor. Repeat, pulling your left leg to your chest. Then pull both legs to your chest.

(e) Sit on the floor, pull your knees to your chest, and bend your head to your knees. Now, gently roll onto your back and then back and forth a few times until you feel all tension disappear from your back.

(f) Lie on your back with your knees elevated and your feet on the floor. Place your hands behind your head. Lift your right leg and place it over your left knee. Use that right leg to pull the left leg toward the floor. You should feel muscles stretching in your lower back and the side of your hip. Repeat, using your left leg to stretch your right side.

14. **Upper Body:** (a) Standing up with your knees bent slightly and your hips directly above your feet, grab a fence, ledge, or railing several feet away. Let your

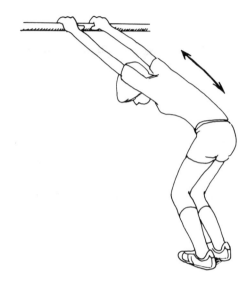

shoulders hang below your hands. By bending your knees a little more or holding on to something a bit taller, you can change the stretch.

(b) Stand with your back a foot or two from a wall or fence. Slowly turn at the waist until you can place your hands on the wall. After 10 to 20 seconds, turn the other way.

(c) Grab both ends of a towel, baseball bat, stick, or string. Keep your arms straight as you slowly raise the object over your head and then lower it behind your back. If you find this difficult, increase the distance between your hands. Conversely, to increase the stretch, move your hands closer together.

15. **Shoulders and arms:** (a) Grab a fence or doorway with your right, outstretched arm. Turn your upper body to the left to stretch the arm and shoulder. By moving your grip up or down the doorway or fence, you can stretch many different muscles.

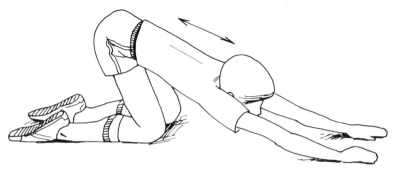

(b) From a kneeling position, bend forward and reach out with one or both arms and press down on the floor gently with your palm(s). A slight movement of your hips can increase or decrease the stretch.

(c) Reach for the ceiling with both arms extended above your head, palms together. Inhale as you reach.

(d) Pull your right elbow across your chest with your left hand. Repeat in the opposite direction.

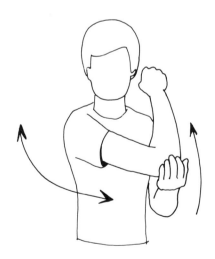

(e) With fingers interlaced and palms turned out, extend your arms in front of your chest. You should feel stretching in all the muscles from the middle of your back to your fingers. Repeat, but this time raise your outstretched arms over your head.

(f) Stretch the muscles in your neck and shoulder by grabbing your left wrist with your right hand behind your back. Pull your left arm diagonally downward as you bend your neck to the right. Repeat the stretch for the right side of your neck and shoulder.

(g) Interlace your fingers, palms inward, behind your back. Turn your elbows inward as you straighten your arms. Repeat, this time lifting your arms. Repeat again with your palms turned outward.

(h) Stretch your forearms and wrists by getting down on four points—knees and palms. Your thumbs should point outward and your fingers toward your knees. To stretch these muscles, keep your palms flat as you lean back raising your shoulders.

16. **Hips and hamstrings (hamstrings may stretch more easily if quadriceps are stretched first):** (a) While lying on your back, pull your lower right leg toward your chest until you feel tension in the upper hamstring. Repeat with the other leg.

(b) Stand with your feet together. Bend at the waist and grab the backs of your lower legs with your hands. Stretch your legs and hips by pulling your upper body downward. Try to reach the floor behind your feet.

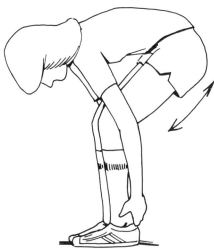

(c) Place your heel on a table, fence, or other object about waist high. Keep your elevated leg straight, and grasp the ankle of this leg with both hands as you bend forward bringing your head toward your knee. Repeat with your other leg.

17. **Groin:** (a) The squat position, commonly seen throughout India in people resting, is good for stretching the groin while resting the lower back.

(b) Place one foot on a table, rail, or fence. Bend the other knee and rest your hands on the floor to provide balance.

(c) Lie on your back with your feet up against a wall. Your buttocks should be only a couple of inches away from the wall. Slowly separate your legs to stretch your groin.

(d) Sit with your legs spread. Lean forward from your hips and reach as far forward as you can, keeping your back straight.

(e) Place the ball of one foot against the edge of a table, railing, or fence. Keep the toes of the other foot pointed straight ahead. Bend the knee of the elevated leg as you move your hips forward, stretching groin and hips. Repeat with your other leg elevated. Repeat again with the down foot pointed to the side instead of straight ahead.

(f) Lie on your back with your knees bent so that the soles of your feet are touching. Let the weight of your knees stretch your groin. Then gently move your knees up and down from this same position.

18. **Quadriceps (front of thigh):** (a) Place one foot behind you in an elevated position supported by the edge of a table, railing, or fence. Stretch the quads

by moving your raised leg forward as you flex your buttocks and bend your other knee. Repeat with your other leg.

(b) Lie on your right side and support your head with your right hand as you might while relaxing. Use your left hand to grab your left ankle and pull it toward your left buttock. At the same time, move your left hip forward. You should feel the quads stretching. Repeat while lying on your left side to stretch your right leg.

(c) Sit with your right leg bent so your right heel is just outside your right hip. You may need to adjust your foot to reduce tension in the ankle, but try to avoid turning your foot outward as much as possible as this will put stress on your knee. Lean back slowly, keeping your right knee

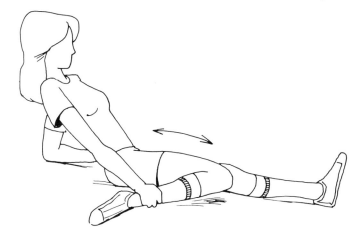

on the floor until you feel tension in the quadriceps. Repeat, stretching your other leg.

(d) While lying on your stomach, reach back and grab your right foot with your left hand, if you can. If not, grab your right foot with your right hand. Pull your foot forward to stretch your quadriceps. Repeat, stretching your other leg.

19. **Achilles tendons, calves and ankles:** (a) From an all-fours position, bring the toes of your left foot even with your right knee, which is on the floor. Raise your left heel slightly; then bring it back down slowly as you press your upper body onto your left thigh. This should stretch your left Achilles tendon and ankle. Repeat with the other leg.

(b) While sitting on the floor, support your raised, bent left leg with your left hand. Use your right hand to rotate your left ankle through its complete range of motion in both directions. Repeat a dozen or so times for each foot. Then gently bend the toes of each foot toward you to stretch the top of your feet.

(c) Use either your hand or a towel around the ball of your foot to pull the toes of your outstretched leg toward your body. This should stretch your calf. Repeat with your other leg. By grabbing the outside of your left foot with your right hand, you can pull your foot inward, stretching the outside of your calf and ankle. Repeat with your right leg.

(d) Stand a foot or so from a fence, wall, tree, goalpost, or other erect support. Lean against it, using your forearms for support. Bend your right leg as you place your left leg behind you in a straightened position with your left foot pointed straight ahead and flat on the floor or ground. Slowly move your hips forward. You should feel your left calf muscle stretching. Repeat, stretching your right calf.

To stretch the Achilles tendon, move your hips downward rather than forward, and bend the knee of your extended leg slightly. Keep your heel on the floor as before.

(e) Stand on a curb or step. Place the ball of your left foot on the edge of the step or curb. Slowly lower your left heel. You may want to hold onto a railing or post to keep your balance. Keep your left leg straight as you stretch the Achilles tendon and ankle. Then repeat with the knee bent slightly. Repeat for the right leg.

Different sports emphasize different muscles and your coaches may recommend particular stretches for the sports you play. If not, you'll be able to tell after a practice session or two which muscles feel tight and need extra stretching.

For more details about stretching, you might like to consult the books by Bob Anderson and Dennis Jackson listed in the Bibliography.

Chapter

**3**

# Building Stronger Muscles

You can move your body because muscles, which connect one bone with another, contract when nerve impulses reach muscle tissue. The nerve impulses cause some of the muscle fibers to contract. This shortens the muscle and makes it thicker. You can feel this when you place one hand on the biceps (upper arm) muscle of your other arm. If your brain now sends nerve messages telling your biceps muscle to raise your lower arm, you will feel the muscle thicken as the fibers shorten, causing your forearm to move toward your shoulder.

Muscles are connected to bones by tendons—gristlelike tissue that is very strong. Tendons connect one end of a muscle to a bone that does not move. This point of connection is called the origin. The muscle connection at the other end is called the insertion. It is connected to the bone that moves.

Skeletal muscles are paired. One muscle, called the flexor, bends a joint; the other muscle straightens the joint and is called an extensor. Your biceps is a flexor muscle. It is paired with the extensor on the back of your upper arm, which is called the triceps. You've felt your biceps when it bent (flexed) your arm. Now feel the triceps on the back of your upper arm contract as you straighten (extend) your arm.

Muscle pairs, such as biceps and triceps, are called antagonists. If one muscle becomes much stronger than its antagonist, the flexibility of the joint controlled by the muscles will be reduced, resulting in a "muscle-bound" condition. To avoid an upset in muscle equilibrium, you should always exercise both members of a muscle pair. You will notice in the muscle-strengthening exercises described later in this chapter that you are asked to exercise both muscles in any pair—biceps and triceps, quadriceps and hamstrings, flexors and extensors.

The chemical reactions involved in muscular contractions are very complex. The net result is that food combines with oxygen, which is carried to the muscle cells by the hemoglobin in red blood cells, to produce carbon dioxide and water. The energy stored in the food is transferred through the work done by the muscle, or it is released as heat.

Some oxygen is stored in muscles. It is combined with the compound myoglobin. Myoglobin is similar to hemoglobin, the iron-rich compound found in red blood cells. Both myoglobin and hemoglobin can attract and hold large amounts of oxygen.

As long as your blood can supply oxygen to your muscles as fast as it is used, you are engaged in *aerobic* exercise. When you increase your exercise to a point where your blood cannot provide oxygen as fast as it is needed, your exercise becomes *anaerobic*. To supply the extra oxygen, your muscles draw on the oxygen held by myoglobin in muscle cells. Once you enter anaerobic exercise, lactic acid builds up in your body. Using the oxygen held by myoglobin creates what is called an *oxygen debt*. It is called a debt because you will have to "pay back" the oxygen borrowed from the myoglobin. This will require heavy breathing for a while to replace the oxygen that was borrowed.

## MAKING MUSCLES GROW

Exercise experts agree that muscles must be worked hard if they are to grow in size and strength. But the experts differ about the best way to exercise.

Many believe that the total work load placed on muscles through many repetitions of an exercise is the way to promote muscle development.

Nautilus Research Director Ellington Darden, among others, maintains that it is the intensity of the work done, not the total amount of work done, that determines muscle strength and growth. He advocates using a load that causes muscle failure after 8 to 12 repetitions. With Nautilus or Universal Gym equipment such an approach is possible because the danger of dropping free weights is avoided.

## STRENGTH TRAINING

There are four training methods presented here to increase your muscle strength: the Nautilus System, the Universal Gym, free weights, and manual resistance exercises. Anyone with a partner can use the manual resistance approach. A set of weights and a barbell are required to do the free weights. The Universal Gym and Nautilus methods require expensive equipment that generally can be found only in gymnasiums or health centers.

The most familiar form of weight training is the use of free weights attached to barbells. These are relatively inexpensive and available in most gymnasiums and many homes. However, this method of strength training can be dangerous unless done carefully. Before you lift any heavy weights, you should practice the technique with small weights. A spotter (an assistant) should work with you, and you should wear shoes to protect your feet from dropped weights and to prevent stubbed toes. Place equal weights on both ends of the bar, and attach the plate collars securely to prevent weights from sliding or falling. Because of the potential danger involved, there should be adult supervision and, of course, you should realize that a weight room is *not* a place where foolish behavior can be tolerated.

With manual resistance strength training, the resistance offered by a partner (spotter) replaces the weights and barbells.

The advantages of strength training through manual resistance are: (1) no equipment is needed; (2) many people can train at the same time; and (3) the speed at which the exercises are performed can be controlled.

It also has two disadvantages, however: (1) two people are required because a spotter (a person not doing exercise) must apply the resistance; and (2) it's impossible to know just how much weight has been "lifted."

If you have access to a Universal Gym or Nautilus machines, learn the techniques needed to use these muscle-strengthening systems before you try to lift heavy weights. Remember, the purpose of weight training is to build, not demonstrate, strength.

Certain rules and techniques apply, whether you use free weights, manual resistance, Nautilus, or a Universal Gym:

1. Warm up before you lift weights. Stretch your muscles and do some exercises—clap-straddles, burpees, running in place, and so forth—to work up a sweat.
2. Exhale when you lift or move weights away from your body. (Blow the weight away!) Inhale while lowering or bringing weight or resistance toward your body. Don't hold your breath while lifting. It can lead to the Valsalva phenomenon—dizziness or loss of consciousness due to the pressure of weight on your body.
3. Lift and return weight or resistance *slowly*. Avoid fast, jerky motions. It should take about two seconds to lift and four seconds to return a weight. Lowering weights is called negative work because the weight is actually doing work on you. Negative work is just as important as lifting.
4. The muscles used in each exercise should move through their full range from maximum contraction to maximum extension.
5. Work the larger muscles first.
6. Concentrate on the muscles being exercised. Relax all others.
7. Always work with another person, a spotter, who will assist you, prevent you from hurting yourself,

provide feedback and encouragement, and push you
to do your best.

**8.** During the off-season, work out three times a week.
Allow at least forty-eight hours between sessions so
your muscles can recover. Work out only once or
twice a week during the season.

**9.** Keep records of the weights you used in each exercise so you can see your progress.

The Nautilus machines are designed to give you a
full workout in 30 minutes or less. Once you are familiar with the technique, you should choose resistances that enable you to do one set of 8 to 12 repetitions before muscle failure; that is, before you can no
longer move your muscles through the full range of the
motion. It's important that you not stop until your
muscles are exhausted. Your spotter should help by
urging you onto the point of muscle failure. Do not
choose resistances you can move only once or twice.
Such weights could tear the muscle or its tendons.

A similar approach (one set of 8 to 12 repetitions)
can be used with the Universal Gym and with manual
resistance. With free weights, it is safer to choose
lighter weights that allow you to do to three sets of 10
repetitions for each exercise.

As your strength grows and you can do more than
12 repetitions, increase the resistances used in each
exercise by about 5 percent.

The exercises listed below are in proper order (large
to small muscle groups). Do no more than twelve such
exercises during any one session.

In manual resistance, it is essential that lifter and
spotter communicate and assume certain responsibil-
ities to obtain maximum benefit from the program. The
lifter should tell the spotter if he or she is offering too
little or too much resistance or pull. Muscular ten-

sion during a muscle exercise should be constant. There should be no momentary rest or relief between repetitions. The lifter should stop only briefly at maximum contraction and extension positions of the muscle. Because a lifter can handle more negative than positive work, the spotter should apply more pressure during the lowering than the lifting phase of the exercise.

The spotter should make sure that the lifter performs the exercise properly. To avoid injury, the resistance during the first several repetitions should be well below the maximum required to do 8 to 12 repetitions.

The amount of resistance needed during the lifting phase will vary because of changes in the leverage of the muscle-bone relationship. Generally, less resistance is required when the joint is flexed and more is needed when it is extended. When properly applied, the resistance will feel constant to the lifter.

During the first few sessions, the spotter should apply less than the maximum resistance the lifter can handle. Allow time for both lifter and spotter to develop the technique.

Avoid applying too much resistance near the muscle's fully stretched position. This is especially true of the neck muscles.

## SPECIFIC EXERCISES

In the exercises presented below, each muscle group exercise can be done using one of the four methods: manual resistance, free weights, Universal Gym, Nautilus.

The manual resistance and free weights methods will be described and illustrated. Exercises for the Nautilus and Universal Gym will be named, but you should ask someone familiar with these machines to show you how to do the exercises if you have access to such equipment.

1. **Muscle group: buttocks, lower back (gluteus maximus, spinal erectors)**

    *Universal Gym*: leg press
    *Nautilus*: hip extension, leg press
    *Free weights*: dead lift and parallel squat

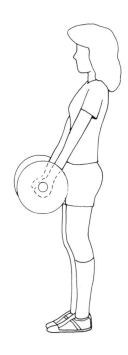

For the dead lift, stand wi'
width, shins close to the bar'
back straight. Grab the bar \
bows outside knees, head u'
and lift by slowly straight'
shoulders back, pause, the
the starting position.

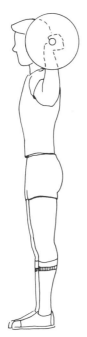

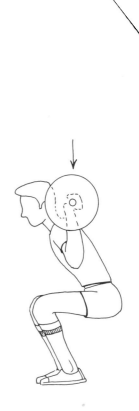

For the parallel squat, have your spotter help place
the barbell on the back of your shoulders. Grip the
bar, feet spread shoulder width, and slowly squat,
keeping the bar over your feet, until your thighs are
parallel with the floor. Pause. Then slowly return to
the starting position. Keep your back straight and
head up throughout the motion. Don't bounce or

end your legs beyond the point where your thighs are parallel to the floor.

Since this exercise begins with negative work, which is easier than positive work (lifting), be sure you do not begin with more weight than you can lift. Have your spotter nearby and start with a light load.

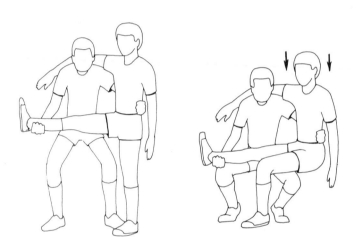

*Manual resistance*: squat

Do one leg at a time for 8 to 12 repetitions if possible. Your spotter should support the leg not being exercised. You can place your arm on your spotter's shoulder for support. From a standing position slowly bend your leg. Keep your foot flat on the floor and your back straight. Continue bending your leg until your thigh is parallel to the floor. Then slowly return to an upright position.

## 2. Muscle group: front of thighs (quadriceps)

*Universal Gym*: leg extension, leg press
*Nautilus*: leg extension, leg press
*Free weights*: leg extension, leg lift
*Manual resistance*: leg extension

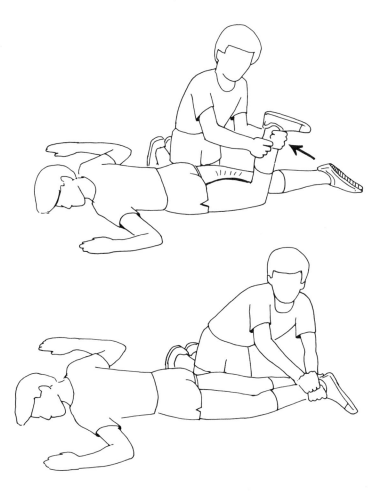

The leg extension exercise is the same for both free weights and manual resistance. Lie on your stomach with one leg flexed upward at the knee as far as it will bend. Your spotter should provide resistance at the front of the ankle of your flexed leg as you straighten the leg to a position beside your unbent leg. After a brief pause, slowly bend the leg back to the starting position while your spotter continues to apply pressure at the front of your ankle. Repeat 8 to 12 times to the point of muscle exhaustion or do three sets of 10 repetitions. Then do the same exercise with your other leg.

Throughout this exercise keep your knee on the floor.

If weights or a sandbag can be attached to your foot, you can sit on a high bench or table and slowly straighten your leg; pause, and then lower it. Again, you can either exercise to exhaustion in 8 to 12 repetitions or do several sets of leg lifts using less weight.

3. **Muscle group: back of thigh (hamstrings—biceps femoris, semitendinosus, semimembranosus)**

*Universal Gym*: leg curl
*Nautilus*: leg curl
*Free weights*: leg curl
*Manual resistance*: leg curl

Again, the free weights and manual resistance exercises are the same. The exercise is similar to the leg extension, but this time you begin with both legs straight. Your spotter applies resistance at the *back* of the ankle as you slowly flex your leg as far as you can. After pausing briefly, you slowly straighten your leg, doing negative work, as your spotter continues to apply pressure at the same place. Your knee should remain against the floor throughout the motion.

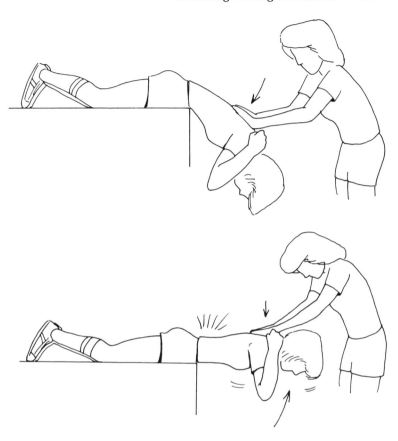

### 4. Muscle group: lower back (sacrospinalis)

*Universal Gym*: leg press
*Nautilus*: hip and back, leg press
*Free weights*: back extension
*Manual resistance*: back extension

The same exercise is used for both the free weights and manual resistance. Lie on your stomach on a table or exercise bench with your upper body extending beyond the table. Begin the exercise with your upper body bent downward, head near the floor. Using your lower back muscles, straighten and arch your back as much as possible. If you can do this easily, your spotter can apply resistance to the upper back.

### 5. Muscle group: calves (gastrocnemius)

*Universal Gym*: heel raise
*Nautilus*: heel raise
*Free weights*: heel raise

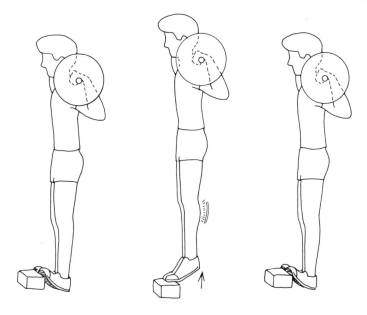

Begin this exercise with a weighted barbell across your shoulders. Grip the bar with both hands after your spotter places it on you. Your feet should be shoulder width apart with the balls of your feet elevated on a thick board or pad, heels on the floor.

Slowly raise your body by standing on your toes until your heels are as far above the floor as possible. After a brief pause, your heels should move slowly back to the floor. Do not rest between raises.

*Manual resistance*: calf raise

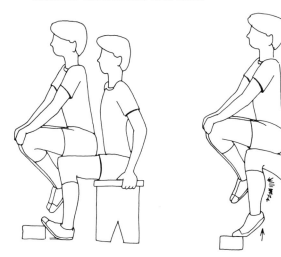

Sit on a stool with your toes on a block of wood, heels on the floor. Your spotter sits on your upper leg or legs. You then raise the spotter by contracting your calf muscles and bringing your heel(s) as high as possible. If you can easily lift your spotter with both legs, have him or her sit on just one leg and do the exercise one leg at a time. As the exercise becomes easier over time, the spotter can hold weights.

## 6. Muscle group: shins (tibialis anterior)

*Universal Gym*: foot flexion
*Nautilus*: foot flexion
*Free weights*: foot flexion
*Manual resistance*: foot flexion

Both the free weights and manual resistance exercise can be done in the same way. Sit on the floor with both legs extended. Point your toes away from your body. The spotter applies resistance to the top of your foot as you flex the foot with your shin muscles until your toes point as nearly as possible toward your body. After a brief pause, slowly return your foot to its initial position.

After the shin muscles of one leg are exhausted, or you have performed several sets of the exercise, repeat the exercise using the other foot.

### 7. Muscle group: biceps, mid-back (latissimus dorsi; rhomboids)

*Universal Gym*: chin-ups, lat pull-down
*Nautilus*: pullover, chin-ups, behind neck pull-downs
*Free weights*: bent-over rowing, bent-over flies, chin-ups
*Manual resistance*: chin-ups

To do chin-ups, which are common to all these modes of exercise, hold on to a high horizontal bar using an underhand grip with both hands. Your body should hang vertically, elbows straight. Slowly raise your body until your chin is above the bar. Pause briefly, and then slowly lower your body to the starting position.

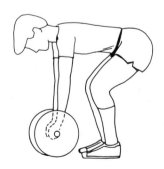 

When you can do 12 repetitions easily, a spotter can apply resistance at your waist or legs.

In bent-over rowing, your back is parallel to the floor and your knees are bent. Use an overhand grip with your hands slightly more than shoulder width apart to raise the weighted bar to your chest. Following a one-second pause, slowly lower the bar to its initial position.

Bent-over flies are performed from the same basic position as bent-over rowing. Instead of a barbell, you should hold a weighted dumbbell in each hand. Slowly lift the weights by raising your arms laterally and upward as far as possible. Then slowly lower the weights to the starting position.

### 8. Muscle group: shoulder (trapezius)

*Universal Gym*: shoulder shrug
*Nautilus*: shoulder shrug
*Free weights*: shoulder shrug

Hold the barbell using an overhand grip, hands shoulder width apart, and arms hanging down. Raise your shoulders as high as possible. Then let your shoulders fall slowly back after a brief pause.

*Manual resistance*: shoulder lift

Your spotter applies resistance to the top of your shoulders while you raise your shoulders as high as possible.

### 9. Muscle group: outer shoulder (deltoids)

*Universal Gym*: seated press, upright row
*Nautilus*: side lateral raise, overhead press
*Free weights*: upright row, lateral raise

To perform the upright row, stand with your feet shoulder width apart. Extend your arms downward holding a barbell with an overhand grip. Keep your hands about 6 inches apart. With a straight back, lift the bar to your chin and then slowly lower it to the starting position.

Do the lateral raise while holding dumbbells. Raise your arms out at your sides until they are parallel to the floor. After a pause, slowly lower them to your sides.

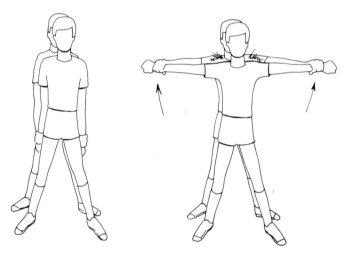

*Manual resistance*: lateral raise

While your spotter applies resistance to the outsides of your wrists, slowly raise your arms out at your sides until they are parallel to the floor. Following a brief pause, lower your arms to your sides as your spotter continues to apply pressure at the same places.

### 10. Muscle group: chest (pectoralis major)

*Universal Gym*: bench press, parallel dip
*Nautilus*: arm cross, decline press, parallel dip
*Free weights*: bent-arm flies

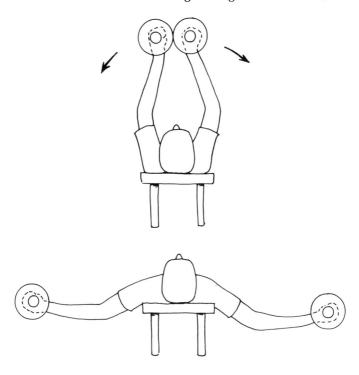

Lie on your back on a bench, knees bent, feet flat on the floor. Hold a pair of dumbbells above your chest, your arms slightly bent. Lower the dumbbells by moving your hands outward and downward, stretching your chest muscles. Then slowly return the weights to the initial position after a brief pause.

*Manual resistance*: bent-arm flies

Lie face up on the floor with your arms out at your sides and bent 90 degrees at the elbows. Your spotter applies resistance at the insides of your elbows as you move your arms slowly upward, finally bringing them together above the middle of your chest.

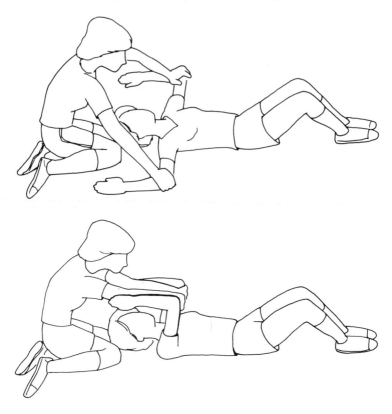

### 11. Muscle group: biceps

*Universal Gym*: chin-up, biceps curl, rowing
*Nautilus*: chin-up, two-arm curl, behind-neck pull-down
*Free weights*: chin-up, biceps curl

To do the biceps curl, grasp the weighted bar with an underhand grip, hands about shoulder width apart. As you stand holding the bar at thigh level, slowly raise the weights to chest level by bending your arms at the elbows using your biceps to provide the lifting force.

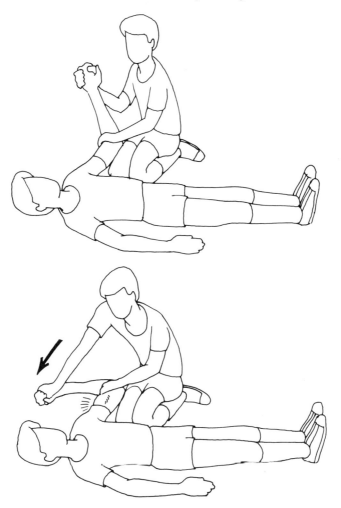

*Manual resistance*: biceps curl

Lie on your back, one arm against the outside of your kneeling spotter's leg and hip. The spotter will use one hand to hold your elbow in place. You will hold the spotter's other hand, which will provide resistance as you slowly bend your arm by contracting your biceps.

**12. Muscle group: triceps**

*Universal Gym*: triceps extension
*Nautilus*: triceps extension
*Free weights*: triceps extension (French curl)

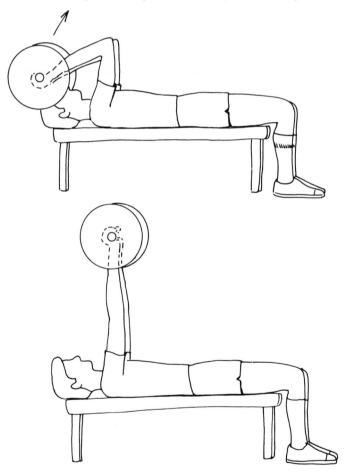

Lie back on a bench, feet flat on the floor. Hold the bar with an overhand grip, hands about a foot apart. The bar should be just above your forehead, held there by your arms bent at the elbows. Contraction of your triceps muscles will straighten your arms raising the weighted bar to a position above your chest. After a brief pause, lower the bar to the starting position. A spotter should be nearby to help in placing and removing the bar.

*Manual resistance*: triceps extension

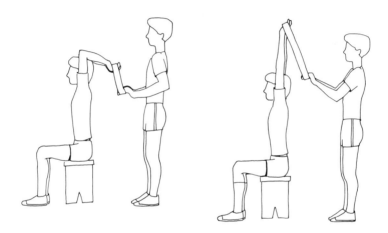

Stand holding a towel behind your neck with your raised arms bent at the elbows. Your spotter also holds the towel, offering resistance as you straighten your arms, raising your hands upward by contracting your triceps muscles.

### 13. Muscle group: forearms (flexors and extensors)

*Universal Gym*: wrist curl, reverse wrist curl
*Nautilus*: wrist curl
*Free weights*: wrist curl, reverse wrist curl

To do the wrist curl, sit on a bench with your feet flat on the floor. Place your forearms on your thighs. Your hands, extending beyond your knees with palms turned upward, hold the weighted bar on your finger tips. Lift the bar by curling your fingertips to bring the bar into your palms. Then, in one slow, smooth, continuous motion, flex your wrists upward as your forearm flexors contract, bringing the weights to their high point. After a pause, slowly return the bar to your fingertips.

Throughout the exercise your forearms should remain against your thighs.

The reverse wrist curl involves the extensor muscles of your forearm. Perform the exercise in the same way as the wrist curl, but hold the bar with an overhand grip so that your palms, below bent wrists, are turned inward, toward your knees. Then slowly curl your wrists upward and backward as far as possible by contracting the forearm extensors.

*Manual resistance*: wrist curl, reverse wrist curl

The exercises are performed in the same way as with free weights except that a towel replaces the barbell. The spotter applies resistance at the ends of the towel.

14. **Muscle group: abdominals (rectus, obliquus, internus, and transversus abdominis)**

    *Universal Gym*: sit-ups, leg raises
    *Nautilus*: abdominal curl
    *Free weights*: sit-ups
    *Manual resistance*: sit-ups

    This exercise is the same for both free weights and manual resistance.

    Lie on the floor, hands folded behind your head, a cushion under your buttocks. Bend your knees, and have your spotter, or some supporting device, hold your feet flat against the floor. Slowly raise your upper body so as to touch your knees with your elbows. Pause. Then slowly return your back to a position just above the floor. Keep your upper back curved and tension on your abdominal muscles.

    If you find this too easy, add resistance by holding a weight in your hands as you do the sit-ups. If you can't do the exercise, place your hands on your stomach instead of behind your head. You'll find it much easier.

15. **Muscle group: neck (sternoclaidomastid, splenius, levator scapulae)**

    *Universal Gym*: neck harness
    *Nautilus*: four-way neck, rotary neck, neck and shoulders
    *Free weights*: neck flexion, neck extension, lateral flexion
    *Manual resistance*: neck flexion, neck extension, lateral flexion

    Because neck exercises are dangerous if too much weight, or sudden pressure, is applied, it is best if you provide the resistance yourself instead of working with a spotter or a free weight.

Throughout all the neck exercises, apply less than maximum resistance. Use the first few repetitions as a warm-up with only minimal resistance.

To do the neck flexion begin with your head tipped back, your neck muscles relaxed. Use your hand on your forehead to provide resistance as you slowly bring your head forward until your chin touches your chest. Pause briefly, then, with the same pressure on your forehead, slowly return to your initial position.

The neck extension exercise begins with your chin on your chest. Hold the back of your head with your hands and use them to provide resistance as you slowly tip your head backward as far as you can. After a one-second pause, return slowly to the chin-on-chest position.

The lateral flexion exercise begins with your head bent (not turned) sideward to the right so that you feel some stretch in the neck muscles. Place your left hand on the left side of your head. Keep your shoulders level as you move your head, eyes looking straight ahead, from above the right shoulder to a position above the left shoulder. Your left hand provides resistance as you move. Following a pause, return to the starting position under similar pressure.

You can repeat the exercise moving your head against resistance from left to right and using your right hand to offer resistance.

*Training is everything.*

# Training for Various Sports

Every sport requires you to use muscles, but in some sports you will use certain muscles more extensively than others. For example, a soccer player must have very strong legs, while a baseball or softball player sets a priority on strong, flexible arms. Both sports require agility, but soccer demands greater stamina and baseball requires a superb eye–hand coordination that is less important in soccer.

Some of the traits required of a good athlete are inherited; there is little you can do about them. Many other physical attributes associated with sports can be developed through training, however. Muscle strength and flexibility, endurance, and specific skills such as dribbling, passing, shooting, throwing, kicking, catching, and jumping can all be improved by practice.

In all sports, the off-season is a good time to work hard on your physical development. Do a strength-training program every other day, preceded by a warm-up and stretching. Practice those skills that you haven't mastered. Be realistic about your ability. Make out a list of your strengths and weaknesses and show it to your coach or a parent. He or she may suggest other areas that need improvement or may feel that you have underestimated your ability in some areas.

## TIPS FOR YOUNG ATHLETES

Whatever sports you participate in, the following tips will help you to become a better athlete and competitor.

- *Hustle*: Being alert, always trying, and never being sluggish often will make up for any skill weaknesses. Pete Rose is a good example of a ball player who made it big by being "Mr. Hustle."
- *Encourage*: Don't criticize your teammates. Everyone makes mistakes; you'll make your share, too. Do you want to hear about them from your fellow players?
- *Be aggressive*: This doesn't mean you should strike your opponents unfairly or hit people in contact sports just for the sake of hitting. It means that you should not hold back in going for a loose ball, running hard, taking that extra base when you have the opportunity, or pursuing someone you may think is faster than you are.
- *Play smart*: Think about the game. What are you going to do if you get the ball? What weaknesses does your opponent have that you can take advantage of? How can you use the clock to your advantage in a close game?
- *Don't argue with or berate the officials*: They may make mistakes, but they're doing their best.

- *Dress properly*: A sloppily dressed team often will play sloppily. Tuck in your shirt, wear your cap properly, keep your socks up, and look sharp.
- *Control your temper*: Don't throw your bat, helmet, racquet, or stick, and never strike an opponent. Loss of emotional control usually is accompanied by loss of physical skill. You won't play as well, and you could be thrown out of the game. Learn to accept setbacks and be determined to do better next time.
- *Wear all required protective equipment*: In addition to the injuries you might incur if you don't wear the proper equipment, the team will suffer if you're unable to play.
- *Develop confidence*: Be so good at certain skills that you know you can perform them successfully even in extremely stressful situations.
- *Cooperate with your coach and fellow players*: A team cannot succeed if it consists of a number of individuals each doing his or her own thing. If you have useful suggestions for another player or for your coach, make them in private, not in front of the entire team.
- *Enjoy your sport*: If you don't enjoy the skills and strategy of the sport you're playing, then find another sport or activity that you like. Success in athletics requires hard work, to be sure; that's part of the benefit. But sports are meant to be enjoyable.

## TRAINING TIPS FOR CERTAIN SPORTS

Stretching, strength training, and running will help you prepare to play any sport. But certain skills, training, and key muscles need special attention in every sport.

Any number of books, including some listed in the

Bibliography, will provide detailed advice and instructions about playing basketball, tennis, volleyball, and other sports. This brief book will be limited to offering some special tips and conditioning suggestions for a few key sports.

## BASKETBALL

Basketball requires great physical stamina and agility as well as supple muscles, low body fat, and considerable body strength. You can gain the endurance required to run up and down the court by playing games regularly and by aerobic and anaerobic running (explained at the end of this chapter). During the season some coaches ask their players to run several miles three times a week in addition to participating in regular practice sessions and games.

During the off-season, you should exercise at least enough to get your heart rate up to 140 to 160 beats a minute for 15 to 20 minutes four or five times each week. You should also participate in some activity that makes you use all of your muscles.

Agility, quickness, and jumping are vitally essential in basketball. The drills described below will help you develop these skills. Do them for short periods at least every other day.

### Agility Drills

- The circle drill can be done with an old tire, a Hula Hoop, or a jump rope laid in a circle. Start with your right foot inside the circle and your left foot outside. Jump, lifting both feet high into the air and to your right, so that you land with your left foot inside the circle and your right foot outside. Immediately jump

again, this time to your left, so that your right foot returns inside the circle. Continue for 30 seconds.

• Begin the bench drill with your right foot on a bench and your left foot on the floor beside the bench. Jump into the air and move across the bench so that you land softly with your left foot on the bench and your

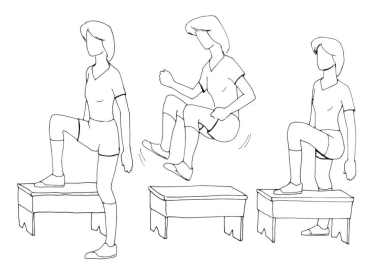

right foot on the floor. Continue jumping back and forth for 30 seconds or until tired.

- Begin two-circle drill with your left foot in the center of one circle and your right foot in the center of a second circle right next to the first. Leap into the air, turn around, and land softly with your feet in opposite circles. Continue to jump and turn for 30 seconds.

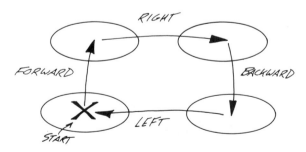

- In the four-circle drill, you jump forward, to your right, backward, and to your left, always landing with both feet inside one of the four circles.

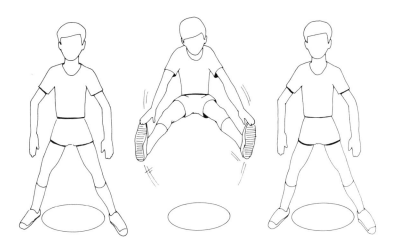

- To perform the straddle jump begin with one foot on each side of a circle. Leap into the air, touch your toes with your hands, and land with your feet straddling the circle again.
- Jumping rope is another simple agility drill that will develop stamina and quick footwork.
- Practice running backwards, feet spread, body low, hands in front of your body. This type of motion is vital to good defensive basketball and football.

## Quickness Drills

- In the ball drill, stand 5 feet or less from a wall and, with a two-hand pass, throw the ball against the wall and then catch it on the rebound.
- For the rebounding drill, stand 5 feet or less from a wall with your back to the wall. Throw the ball over your head up against the wall. Jump, turn in midair, and catch the ball facing the wall.

- In "call ball," a line of players stand with their backs to another player who has a ball. The passer calls the name of one of the players as he or she throws the ball. The player named must turn quickly and catch the ball.
- "Hear ball" is similar to "call ball" except that all the players turn when they hear the ball bounce. The passer delivers a bounce pass to anyone in the line.
- In "circle catch," six players form a 20-foot-diameter circle around a single player at the center of the circle. The player in the center turns slowly. When he faces any one of the six on the circumference, that player may pass the ball to him or her. If the player catches the ball, he or she may pass it back and begin turning in the opposite direction.

## *Jumping Drills*

- Jump as high as you can and touch a point on a wall. Mark a point two inches above the point you touched. Continue jumping until you reach the higher point. Next time set the mark two inches higher.
- From a squatting position, leap as high into the air as you can. Try to land as softly as you can. After 10 jumps, rest for one minute; then do two more sets of 10 jumps with a one-minute rest between.
- From a bench 2 or 3 feet high, jump to the floor. Land as softly as possible and immediately jump as high as you can. Do three sets of 10 jumps with brief rest periods between sets.
- Here's a great drill for the summer. In water that is shoulder deep when you are crouched, jump as high as you can. Repeat 10 times as rapidly as you can. Rest and repeat the drill until you're tired. Many coaches believe this drill improves nerve–muscle coordination because the reduced resistance due to water's buoyancy allows muscles to contract faster.

Repetition of this drill, in effect, "programs" the muscles to contract faster.

- When you must go upstairs, don't walk, hop! Hop up steps first on one leg, then on the other. As your strength grows, you'll be able to hop up steps two at a time. But *don't* hop downstairs.

Most important, keep shooting! The name of the game is putting the ball through the hoop. Work on your best shot and perfect it. Practice free throws, especially when you're tired; that's when, late in the contest, key foul shots can often win a game.

## Stretching Specials

These stretches, from Chapter 2, are particularly important for basketball players: 2, 3, 4, 6, 10, 14a, 16c, and 19d.

Players of other sports, such as volleyball, that require agility, quickness, and jumping can benefit from the drills described above. So, too, can baseball players who must jump for hard-hit liners; soccer players who need to leap from a crowd to head a ball; or football ends and defensive backs who need to jump high in the air to snare passes and run backwards.

## BASEBALL

Hitting a fast-moving ball in such a way as to change its direction radically requires outstanding eye–hand coordination. And the ability to field hard-hit balls and make accurate throws requires exceptional agility and arm strength.

Most of the running done in baseball covers short distances so aerobic running is not very important in baseball or softball. But speed is important, and so are supple muscles and mental alertness. Maintain your wind by running about eight 50-yard sprints at ¾ speed with no rest between sprints.

Before throwing or running, you should do these stretching exercises from Chapter 2: 1 to 12, 14c, 15b, 15d, 15e, 15f, 15h, 16b, 16c, 17d, 18b, 18d, 19a, and 19d.

Each day you should work on your agility by throwing, playing pepper, fielding grounders and flies, and running bases. Start throwing with other players spread about 20 feet apart. Gradually increase the distance as your arm loosens.

## Tips for Baseball Players

- Run out all balls hit. Don't watch the ball from home plate or as you move toward first. Your first-base coach will tell you what to do.
- Tag up on all foul balls and flies.
- With a player on second, try to hit to the right side.
- Remember, an outfielder can overcall an infielder, and a center fielder can overcall other outfielders.
- The player on deck should signal a runner approaching home to slide or stay up.
- With a runner on third and less than two out, an outfielder should not catch a long fly that is definitely foul. If caught, the runner may tag and score.
- With a player who can win the game on third, a visiting team's outfield should play shallow to prevent a Texas leaguer. A long fly will produce a run anyway.
- With two out and a 3–2 count on the batter, infield-

ers should throw to first, because all base runners will be going on the pitch.

- If you are asked to bunt with a runner on first, push the ball along the first-base line. With runners on first and second, bunt toward third.
- With two out and a runner on second, infielders play deep to reduce the likelihood of a ground single or Texas leaguer that could allow the runner to score.
- If you're on third and a teammate is on first with one out, you should break on any ground ball that could be a double-play ball. If the opposition plays to cut you off at home, get in a run-down so that each of the other two players can move up an extra base.
- If you're to pitch, take 20 minutes to warm up; then relax for 5 to 10 minutes, keeping your arm covered, before taking the mound.
- If you're a catcher, always wear a mask while warming the pitcher.
- Always wear a batting helmet at the plate and on the base paths.
- As an infielder, watch for runners who miss a base or who leave too soon when they tag up. Appeal before the next pitch.
- The catcher should tell an infielder fielding a bunt where to throw the ball.
- If a runner breaks for the next base while the pitcher is on the rubber, the pitcher should step off the rubber to avoid a balk call, and then throw ahead of the runner.
- With a runner on third, the shortstop and second baseman should back up the pitcher on throws from the catcher.
- To make the plays required of a good ball player, you should be alert but not tense. Tension can interfere with your agility and prevent the smooth coordination that baseball and softball require.

During the off-season, ball players should run at least a mile three times a week, and run ten sprints, preferably uphill, during the same workouts.

In their weight training, they should work particularly hard on wrist curls and reverse wrist curls. A weight or bag of sand tied to the center of a broom handle can be used in place of a weighted barbell.

To maintain the eye–hand coordination so vital to playing ball, it's good to play other sports such as basketball, squash, and handball that demand the same skill.

As the season approaches, in addition to your regular exercise, try to play pepper for 10 minutes each day; work on catching and throwing quickly; swing a bat 50 times a day. Increase the number each day until you reach 100 swings.

During the season limit your participation in other sports that may affect your swing, coordination, or your ability to see the ball. Above all, concentrate on watching the ball. The player who can see the ball from the pitcher's hand to the bat is going to be a good hitter.

## WRESTLING

Because of the variety of holds involved in wrestling, all of your muscles must be strong and supple if you want to succeed in this sport. Stretching and weight training are essential for success. You will also benefit from some of the agility drills described for basketball players. In addition, both aerobic and anaerobic running (sprints) should be part of your training if you are a wrestler.

The most difficult part of wrestling for many participants is the need to diet. Many wrestlers foolishly
starve themselves, dehydrate their bodies by taking
water pills or laxatives, or even induce vomiting in order to lose weight. Such methods produce physical
and mental problems that are counterproductive.

The only sensible way to lose body fat is to ingest
less energy in food than you expend in exercise. But it
is vital that your diet include some foods from all nutrient groups (see Chapter 5) so that your body gets all
the necessary nutrients. The extra energy will come
from body fat.

Eat only one average serving of each food at each
meal. Eat slowly and chew your food thoroughly.
Avoid such fatty foods as butter, mayonnaise, oils, and
cooking fats, as well as desserts and other sweets.

Eat a good breakfast and don't skip meals. Don't do
what I've seen some young wrestlers do—skip breakfast, lunch, and all of dinner except dessert.

Don't get caught up in diet drugs or exercise and diet
gimmicks. A vitamin supplement won't hurt you, but
an excess of any one or all vitamins is worthless.


## FOOTBALL

Football players can benefit from weight training,
stretching, agility drills, and anaerobic as well as
aerobic running. Some people think that endurance is
not vital to football because there's a huddle between
plays. However, the huddle is short-lived, and coaches
encourage players to run to and from the huddle. Further, there are often times, near the end of a half, when
a team will call plays from the line of scrimmage to
save time.

Because the shoulder and neck are used so much in blocking and tackling, you need to work especially hard to strengthen these muscles. If you don't have access to a Nautilus or Universal Gym, ask your coach for some neck-strengthening exercises. Be sure you know how to do these exercises safely; they can be dangerous if not done with care.

You should also work hard on your quadriceps, because they govern the movement of your knee—a joint that is particularly subject to injury in football.

## GOLF

If you are a golfer you can strengthen your hands during the off-season by squeezing a rubber ball. Wrist curls and reverse wrist curls will strengthen your forearm muscles, and aerobic running will help you develop endurance.

During the season, running will help you stay in shape, and you should practice your putts and drives. Fingertip push-ups are good for developing hand strength. Keep your palms off the ground.

Many golf coaches oppose weight training except as a way to repair damaged muscles. Upper torso development, they feel, inhibits the body turns so essential in golf.

There are some no-nos in golf that you as a young player should be aware of:

- Don't talk or stand near another golfer while he or she is making a stroke or putt. Stand quietly and still, well away from the ball. Your shadow should not fall on the path of the ball being played.

- Never walk across the line of another player's putt.
- Don't hold up players behind you. Let them play through if your match is going slowly.
- Don't drop your bag on the putting green or where it can interfere with another's play.
- Replace any divots made by your shots, and fill any holes you make in a bunker.
- Don't shoot into an area where other golfers are still playing. Be sure they are well out of range before you shoot.

## HOCKEY

The fundamental skill for hockey is the ability to skate, and every young player should skate as much as possible. Learn to skate backwards with the same ease that you move forward.

Hip skating (skating without lifting your blades from the ice) will make your hips work harder and strengthen them. To improve your agility, skate around obstacles on the ice. Stop-and-go skating will build endurance and leg strength while improving both your positive and negative acceleration.

With another player, you can practice passing as you skate.

To develop the strong hands and wrists you will need to control a stick you can do wrist curls and reverse wrist curls. Squeezing a rubber ball while you read or watch television will help, too. A good way to strengthen your fingers, hands, and wrists is to twist a towel in your hands.

An off-season sport such as baseball, handball, tennis, squash, volleyball, or basketball will help you to maintain the eye–hand coordination so vital to hockey. Do distance running to develop endurance, and uphill sprints to build leg strength. Cycling is good for hockey legs, too.

## Tips for Hockey Players

- When stickhandling, keep your head up and your arms away from your body so as to increase your range of motion with the puck. "Cushion," don't slap, the puck with your stick. Black tape on your stick will improve your puck control and help to hide the puck.
- Remember, passing moves the puck faster than stickhandling does.
- Skate with your stick on the ice. That's where the puck is.
- Draw an opponent to you before you pass.
- Learn to make and receive passes on both sides of your stick.
- Don't pass across your goal.
- Shoot low and look for rebounds; don't stand and watch.
- Try to shoot on the move so the goalie can't set up.
- On face-offs, watch the referee's hand that holds the puck.
- On face-offs in your defensive zone, cover each opponent. Think defense!
- When a defenseman moves across your opponent's blue line, a forward should cover the point.
- Never go three abreast into the offensive end. Use a trailing forward to whom you can pass or who can cover defensively if a pass is intercepted.
- When checking, watch your opponent's midsection; don't be fooled by clever stickhandling.
- Stay low on body checks.

- Cover the men in front of your net; they're the most dangerous.
- Don't allow opponents to screen your goalie.
- Try to force opponents at the blue line. Don't let them skate easily into your defensive zone.
- Goalies should avoid rebounds by covering loose pucks; always play the puck from the ice up; watch for opponents who "telegraph" their shots; talk to and direct your teammates; and try to stay upright. Keep your body off the ice.

## SKIING

Good ski coaches often give this advice: "Don't try to ski competitively unless you are in good physical condition."

Cross-country running is a good off-season sport for a skier, because it builds leg strength and endurance. Certainly a skier should be able to run 4 or 5 miles every other day before the season begins.

Agility is essential to you as a skier, so you will find the drills described for basketball useful. Work in gymnastics, too, can help develop agility.

Weight training is good for skiers, especially in developing calf muscles, quadriceps, and the antagonists of these muscles. You can strengthen your middle- and upper-body muscles through strength training or by doing sit-ups, push-ups, and chin-ups. Repetitive sets rather than lifting to exhaustion with 8 to 12 repetitions is probably best, because you don't want muscle mass.

Before skiing, it is essential that your Achilles tendons, quadriceps, and hamstrings be well stretched.

## SOCCER

You will need endurance, agility, speed, and leg strength to play soccer; hence, running (both distance and sprints), agility drills, and strength training should be part of your pre-season routine. You should also work on skills, such as dribbling, head juggling, thigh juggling, foot juggling, passing at a target using both feet, and heading a ball against a wall. With a partner, you can practice throw-ins, passing as you run, and see how long the two of you can keep the ball in the air by kicking and heading. You can also chip to each other over an obstacle such as a bush; punt or drop-kick to each other; and practice penalty shots.

### Tips for Soccer Players

- On offense, stay on your side of the field, keep the ball moving, and look for openings through which you can receive a pass.
- When kicking, keep your head down and your eyes on the ball. The knee of your kicking foot should be over the ball at the time your foot hits the ball.
- Head the ball with your forehead, but let power come from your entire upper body, from waist to head.
- Trap the ball before you try a chip or a long pass.
- Dribble with your head up, and don't dribble if you can make a pass.
- Put your body into all shots, and aim low; goalies hate to "hit the dirt."
- On throw-ins, keep both of your feet on the ground *behind* the line. After you've thrown, step into the field, ready to receive a pass.
- On defense, talk to your teammates. Find out who's covering an unguarded opponent. Call for a switch if an opponent has beaten one of your players.

- When tackling, concentrate on watching the ball, not your opponent.
- As a goalie, you should direct the defense. Once you decide to go for a ball, don't hesitate.
- On penalty kicks, be ready to rebound.
- In your movements, try to create open spaces for your teammates.

## TENNIS

If you are a tennis player, basketball is a good off-season sport for you because it involves the quick starts and stops so essential to good tennis, as well as the eye–hand coordination, quickness, agility, and endurance that tennis requires. Certainly you can use many of the drills suggested for basketball players.

Uphill sprints followed by a one-mile run can improve your leg strength and endurance.

Stomach muscles are very much involved in tennis movements; therefore, you should do sit-ups routinely and in great number. Wrist curls, reverse curls, fingertip push-ups, and squeezing a rubber ball are useful for developing hand and wrist strength. Many coaches oppose intensive weight training for tennis; they feel that muscle mass inhibits the flexibility so essential in serving and stroking a tennis ball.

## VOLLEYBALL

As a volleyball player, you will benefit from the agility, quickness, jumping, and endurance training suggested for basketball players.

You can use a basketball backboard to practice volleyball control. Throw the ball up and hit it off the backboard. On the return, bounce it into the air with your arms. When it comes down, hit it against the backboard again.

Another good exercise is to bounce the ball over your head with your arms. Give it enough backward velocity and height so that you can turn, run after it, and bounce it again with your arms. See how long you can keep the ball in the air. With a partner to throw to you, you can also practice spiking the ball. A net isn't essential. You can use a rope or pieces of cloth tied together at net height.

## ROWING

Total body strength and endurance are essential for an oarsman. It also helps if you are tall and carry very little body fat. Strength training, distance running, and uphill running can help your development during the off-season.

Continue weight training and running in the pre-season, but also begin using an ergometer (if one is available) and a rowing machine. Cycling, marathon bar work, and body circuits should also be part of your routine.

Marathon bar work involves using a barbell, weighted to one-third your body weight, to do the following lifting exercises (see Chapter 3):

- Biceps curl
- Dead lift
- Upright row
- Bent-over rowing

- Burpee-bars (burpee with barbell in hand—see Chapter 2)
- Military press (begin on your back with the barbell on your chest; lift bar until arms are straight, and return)
- Parallel squat

Do 10 repetitions of each exercise without rest between the seven exercises. Do four to six sets, but don't work longer than 20 minutes.

The body circuit includes the following exercises:

1. Harvard step test, 4 minutes: Record pulse (see Chapter 7).
2. Push-ups: Do as many as possible in 30 seconds.
3. Sit-ups: Do as many as possible in 30 seconds.
4. Burpees: Do as many as possible in 30 seconds.
5. Shoulder stretch: Do stretch 14c (Chapter 2).
6. Chin-ups: Do as many as possible in 30 seconds.
7. Chest lifts: Lie on your stomach with your hands locked behind your neck; anchor your feet and raise your chest as high as possible. Repeat as often as possible over a 30-second period.
8. Bends: Hold a 15-pound dumbbell in each hand as you move from an erect stance to one in which your thighs are parallel to the floor. Keep your knees close together. Repeat as often as you can in 30 seconds.
9. Rest for 2 minutes.

Try to do three sets. Watch your progress by recording your pulse counts after the intervals specified.

A week-long schedule might look like this:

- Monday: strength training—three sets of 10 repetitions (see Chapter 3)—plus a 30-minute run
- Tuesday: marathon bar (1 hour) plus 20 minutes of sprinting

- Wednesday: strength training plus a 30-minute run
- Thursday: four to six sets of body circuits plus 20 minutes of sprinting
- Friday: strength training plus a 30-minute run
- Saturday: marathon bar (30 minutes) plus three or four sets of body circuits
- Sunday: a long run (1 hour) or bike ride (2 to 3 hours)

## TRACK AND FIELD

All athletes require strong legs, and so running is basic to all sports. During a long run you should be relaxed. Let your body lean forward slightly but keep your head up. Your hands and arms should be relaxed, elbows bent so as to form an angle of about 100 degrees. For balance your arms must swing some. On the back swing, your hands shouldn't go beyond your hips; on the forward swing, let them pump toward the center of your body. Your toes should point straight ahead, and you should travel in a straight line.

If you are just beginning to run, start by jogging for a while. When you can run a mile with little difficulty, you can begin to increase both speed and distance. Don't try anaerobic running (sprints) until you've been running aerobically for at least a month.

Your body becomes more efficient with use—that is, you will require less oxygen to do the same amount of work. This is the result of more red blood cells to carry oxygen, better circulation, more air inhaled with each breath, and better heart efficiency. Repeated aerobic running, therefore, allows you to run the same distance at greater speed without incurring an oxygen debt.

Anaerobic training will enable you to build up larger oxygen debts, which in turn will enable you to run a more effective sprint at the end of a long race. Find out how fast you can run an 880-yard (½-mile) sprint. Use that pace to run ten 440-yard sprints with 3-minute rest periods between runs. You can also run sprints of 50 to 300 yards with full recovery between sprints. Relay races will break the boredom of sprinting if there are enough people to run them.

If you can do as much anaerobic work on day two as you did on day one, you can increase your anaerobic work. If you can't do as much on the second day, you probably did too much the previous day and should cut back.

Once you're into anaerobic as well as aerobic running, you can vary your running routine with uphill runs, aerobic runs, and anaerobic running. If you're a distance runner, try to do your aerobic running at a pace just below the point where your running becomes anaerobic. If you can run a 6-minute mile aerobically, but a 5:40 mile is an anaerobic effort that leaves you puffing, then do long runs at a 6-minutes-per-mile pace.

Serious runners should read the books by Lydiard, Sheehan, Valentine, Fixx, and Parker listed in the Bibliography.

## Tips for Runners

- Always pass competitors on straightaways. You have to run farther if you pass on curves.
- Once you go into your kick, don't look back.
- If you sprint well, delay your kick as long as possible. If you don't have a good sprint, force your competitors earlier in the race.

- Run against good competition. Don't enter races that you know you can win easily.
- Don't panic if someone starts with a swift pace; he or she will be tired when it's time for a kick. Know your best pace and stick with it.
- Wear good running shoes with thick, padded soles and heels that are higher than soles to reduce strain on your Achilles tendon. Have them fitted in the store.
- Dress warmly if you run in cold weather. Keep your ears, face, and hands covered.
- Use Vaseline to lubricate areas subject to chafing.
- When you run, let your feet roll from heel to toe so that you push off your toes. Don't run on your toes over appreciable distances. It can lead to sore calves and strain on the Achilles tendon.
- After a run, cool down by jogging, walking, and stretching until your heart rate is within 20 beats per minute of its normal rate.
- If you run on a road at night or early in the morning, wear a reflective vest and run facing traffic.
- If your sprint time for a 200-yard dash is consistently 26 seconds or higher, you're probably going to do better as a distance runner than as a sprinter.
- Don't think too much when you run. Try to run naturally or you may end up like the centipede:

> The centipede was happy quite
> Until a toad in fun,
> Said, "Pray, which leg goes after which?"
> That worked her mind to such a pitch,
> She lay distracted in a ditch,
> Not knowing how to run.

'Tis not the meat, but 'tis the
appetite
Makes eating a delight.

# What Do Athletes Eat?

Do outstanding athletes achieve stardom by eating the right foods? Probably not; the diets of athletes are as diverse as those of any other group of individuals. But athletes, like everyone else, must be certain to follow a diet that includes foods from each of the following groups:

1. Meat and other high-protein foods
2. Citrus fruit
3. Dark green or yellow vegetables
4. Other fruits and vegetables
5. Milk
6. Breads, cereals, and other starch-containing foods
7. Fats

A more detailed view of each of these food groups is presented below together with the energy content in calories of an average serving.

    1.   An ounce (28.4 grams) of lean meat contains 7 grams (g) of protein and 5g of fat. It is equivalent

to an ounce of beef, lamb, pork, liver, chicken, or fish, an egg, a hot dog, three sardines, a slice of cheese, five shrimps or clams, one-quarter cup of cottage cheese, or two tablespoons of peanut butter (75 calories).

2. A serving of citrus fruit is one-half cup. It contains 10g of carbohydrate. Oranges, grapefruit, lemons, limes, and their juices are citrus fruits, but strawberries, cantaloupe, and tomato juice are good substitutes that are rich in vitamin C (40 calories).

3. Dark green or yellow vegetables contain 7g of carbohydrate and 2g of protein per half-cup serving. They include such foods as broccoli, carrots, lettuce, peppers, pumpkin, tomatoes, watercress, winter squash, the greens of beets, turnips, and dandelions, chard, kale, and spinach (35 calories).

4a. A half-cup serving of other fruits contains 10g of carbohydrate. These fruits include apples, apricots, bananas, blueberries, cherries, dates, figs, grapes, mangoes, peaches, pears, pineapples, plums, prunes, raspberries, and watermelon (40 calories).

4b. A half-cup serving of other vegetables contains 7g of carbohydrate and 2g of protein. The vegetables included are asparagus, beets, cabbage, cauliflower, cucumbers, eggplant, green beans, mushrooms, onions, peas, summer squash, and turnips (35 calories).

5. A cup of milk contains 12g of carboyhdrate, 8g of protein, and 10g of fat. Skim milk has very little fat and hence contains about 90 fewer calories per cup than whole milk. A cup of buttermilk, one-quarter cup of powdered milk and one-half cup of evaporated milk are the nutritional equivalents of one cup of milk (170 calories).

6. A slice of bread contains 15g of carbohydrate and

2g of protein. Its equivalents include half a hot dog bun, a cup of popcorn, a roll or muffin, one-half cup of cooked cereal, three-quarters cup of cold cereal, one-half cup of macaroni, noodles, or spaghetti, one-half cup of dried peas or beans, one-quarter cup of baked beans, one potato, an ounce of potato chips, eight french fries, one small slice of pizza, one piece of corn bread, one-quarter cup of yams, or one-half cup of ice cream (70 calories).

7. A teaspoonful of fat is about 5 grams—the amount of fat contained in a slice of bacon, a teaspoon of butter, cream, margarine, mayonnaise, or cooking oil, or in a tablespoon of cream cheese or French dressing (45 calories).

Here are some typical balanced daily meals for a 2500-, 2700-, and 3000-calorie diet. (If you are training hard, you may need to eat much more. If you are inactive because of an injury or for some other reason, you should eat less.) All these diets contain adequate amounts of vitamins, minerals, and proteins, but if you have to restrict your food intake, you may want to take a vitamin and mineral supplement.

### 2500-CALORIE DIET

| Food Group | Amount per Day | Food Content (Vitamins and Minerals Not Listed) | Calories |
|---|---|---|---|
| (1) Meat | 5 oz. | 35g protein, 25g fat | 375 |
| (2) Citrus fruit | ½ cup | 10g carbohydrate | 40 |
| (3) Green or yellow vegetables | ½ cup | 7g carbohydrate, 2g protein | 35 |

## 2500-CALORIE DIET

| Food Group | Amount per Day | Food Content (Vitamins and Minerals Not Listed) | Calories |
|---|---|---|---|
| (4) Other fruits and vegetables | 1 cup | 20g carbohydrate | 80 |
| (5) Milk | 4 cups | 48g carbohydrate, 32g protein, 40g fat | 680 |
| (6) Breads, etc. | 13 servings | 195g carbohydrate, 26g protein | 910 |
| (7) Fats | 10 teaspoons | 50g fat | 450 |

## 2700-CALORIE DIET

| Food Group | Amount per Day | Food Content (Vitamins and Minerals Not Listed) | Calories |
|---|---|---|---|
| (1) Meat | 5 oz. | 35g protein, 25g fat | 375 |
| (2) Citrus fruit | ½ cup | 10g carbohydrate | 40 |
| (3) Green or yellow vegetables | ½ cup | 7g carbohydrate, 2g protein | 35 |
| (4) Other fruits and vegetables | 1½ cups | 30g carbohydrate | 120 |
| (5) Milk | 4 cups | 48g carbohydrate, 32g protein, 40g fat | 680 |
| (6) Breads, etc. | 16 servings | 240g carbohydrate, 32g protein | 1120 |
| (7) Fats | 10 teaspoons | 50g fat | 450 |

## 3000-CALORIE DIET

| Food Group | Amount per Day | Food Content (Vitamins and Minerals Not Listed) | Calories |
|---|---|---|---|
| (1) Meat | 7 oz. | 49g protein, 35g fat | 525 |
| (2) Citrus fruit | ½ cup | 10g carbohydrate | 40 |
| (3) Green or yellow vegetables | ½ cup | 7g carbohydrate, 2g protein | 35 |
| (4) Other fruits and vegetables | 1½ cups | 30g carbohydrate | 120 |
| (5) Milk | 4 cups | 48g carbohydrate, 32g protein, 40g fats | 680 |
| (6) Breads, etc. | 18 servings | 270g carbohydrate, 32g protein | 1260 |
| (7) Fats | 10 teaspoons | 50g fat | 450 |

The chart below shows the number of calories of energy required each day per pound of body weight for boys and girls of different ages. The numbers are based on moderate amounts of exercise. If you are in heavy training, you should eat more. If you are not active or are overweight, eat less.

## CALORIES PER POUND PER DAY

| Age | Boys | Girls |
|---|---|---|
| 10−12 | 32 | 29 |
| 12−14 | 24 | 23 |
| 14−18 | 23 | 21 |

A moderately active, average fifteen-year-old girl who weighs 100 pounds will need to eat 2100 calories per day (100 pounds × 21 cal./lb./day) to maintain her weight. If she is still growing, she will need more food to provide the energy to build new tissue.

Because people differ in the efficiency with which they use the food they eat, an occasional look at your body in a mirror is the best way to tell if you are too fat or too thin. Adjust your food intake on the basis of what you see.

If you exercise vigorously on a regular basis, you need about ⅓ gram of protein per pound of body weight to replace protein lost in tissue breakdown each day. This amounts to only 70g for even a 200-pound athlete. Since the diets of most Americans include plenty of protein, the additional energy that active athletes require can come from inexpensive carbohydrates such as breads, cereals, and other fruits and vegetables rather than from expensive protein-rich foods.

If you keep a record of what you eat, you can easily determine your energy intake. A sample diet for one day is provided below. It shows how you can use the information in the tables above to calculate your energy intake in calories. For example, a poached egg is a meat (group 1) food, equivalent to an ounce of lean meat, which holds 75 calories of energy. There is only one item—cake—for which you will need additional information. (See the table of energy values for desserts on page 90.)

## SAMPLE ONE-DAY DIET

| Breakfast | Calories |
|---|---|
| ½ cup orange juice | 40 |
| 1 poached egg | 75 |
| 2 slices toast | 140 |
| 1 teaspoon butter | 45 |
| 1 cup milk | 170 |

| Lunch | |
|---|---|
| 2 hot dogs | 150 |
| 2 buns | 140 |
| 1 teaspoon margarine | 45 |
| 1 cup milk | 170 |
| 1 apple | 40 |

| Dinner | |
|---|---|
| 6 oz. lamb | 450 |
| ½ cup dark green salad | 35 |
| 1 tablespoon French dressing | 45 |
| 1 cup peas | 70 |
| 1 large potato | 140 |
| 2 rolls | 140 |
| 3 cups water | 0 |
| 2 cups milk | 340 |
| 1 slice frosted cake | 400 |
| 1 cup ice cream | 140 |
| Total = | 2775 |

If you are an active athlete, you can eat desserts to supply some of your energy needs (see the table below). However, if you are overweight, avoid sugar-laden desserts. Sugar is not harmful, as long as it doesn't remain in your mouth to promote cavities, but it contains none of the vitamins or minerals that other foods offer.

## SUGAR-RICH FOODS

| Dessert | Calories |
|---------|----------|
| Milk shake | 400 |
| Malted milk shake | 500 |
| Ice cream soda | 250 |
| Sundae | 300 |
| Pie (1 slice) | 300 |
| Frosted cupcake | 200 |
| Frosted cake (1 slice) | 400 |
| Brownie | 150 |
| Cookie | 120 |
| Pound cake (1 slice) | 130 |
| Peanuts (small bag) | 150 |
| Doughnut | 130 |

# DIETING TO LOSE WEIGHT

If the food you eat contains more energy than you expend in exercise, growth, heat production, and maintaining life functions, you will gain weight. The excess food is stored as fat. This fat tends to collect in certain parts of the body—thighs, abdomen, upper arms, and buttocks. It also is deposited between muscle fibers where it impedes free movement of these muscles and therefore reduces efficiency of movement.

The best way to shed excess fat is to exercise and reduce your food intake. Fad diets based on a single food and crash diets that rely on starvation can be dangerous. Your physician can provide a diet that is nutritious yet low in calories. Often a change in your style of eating rather than in the foods you eat will be enough to bring about loss of weight.

Here are two breakfasts that contain similar foods, but notice the difference in the way these foods are prepared:

1. On half a toasted English muffin place a slice of Canadian bacon and one poached egg. Add pepper to taste.
2. On half a buttered toasted English muffin, place a slice of bacon and one egg fried in bacon fat. Add salt and pepper to taste.

The second breakfast contains about 100 calories more than the first. The muffin was buttered; fatty bacon rather than lean Canadian bacon was used; the egg was cooked in fat rather than water, which has no calories, and was seasoned with salt, which helps hold water in the body.

If you have a computer in your home or at school, you might like to examine or use such software programs as "Health-Aide" (Knassos, Inc.). These programs will plan diets, store menus (of food, not computer menus), calculate budgets, prepare shopping lists, and determine the exercise you need to burn off various quantities of energy. From data you provide about your height, weight, sex, and age, the programs will determine your food needs and establish diets that, if followed, will enable you to lose weight while eating nutritious meals.

Such computerized diets are based on mathematical formulas that may not take into account your particular individual nature, however. Consequently, it's best to see your physician before you embark on a diet prescribed by a computer.

## DIETING TO GAIN WEIGHT

Though excess food is stored as fat in our bodies, some body fat is necessary. It covers nerves and cell membranes, and it cushions vital internal organs. It is depot fat that collects in thighs, hips, abdomen, and buttocks, and subcutaneous (under-the-skin) fat that hinders movement, puts an additional burden on the heart, and raises blood pressure. Beyond the small amount of essential fat, any increased body weight on an athlete should be in the form of muscle tissue.

To promote muscle development, muscles must be stimulated by exercise. In addition, protein must be available to form new muscle cells, and there must be periods of rest to allow exercised muscles to recover. Since a pound of muscle is only about 20 percent protein (two-thirds is water) and requires about 600 calories to grow, increasing muscle tissue by one pound a week would require only an additional 15g of protein and 100 calories each day. As I mentioned earlier, most Americans eat an excess of protein, so a protein supplement is not required.

To lose fat, while growing muscle, you should reduce your food intake so that it is about 500 calories below your energy needs. The extra 500 calories will be supplied by your body fat.

The table below gives you some idea of the energy you will burn up in various sports.

## ENERGY BURNED UP IN SPORTS

| Sport | Calories per hour |
| --- | --- |
| Cross-country skiing | 900 |
| Downhill skiing | 600 |
| Jogging | 600 |
| Ballet | 600 |
| Basketball | 400 |
| Tennis (singles) | 400 |
| Field hockey | 375 |
| Swimming | 300 |

**ENERGY BURNED UP IN SPORTS**

| Sport | Calories per hour |
| --- | --- |
| Bicycling | 300 |
| Golf | 200 |
| Softball | 100 |

Actually, exercise raises your overall metabolic rate as much as 50 percent so that you can lose weight much more easily if you exercise. Furthermore, your metabolism does not return to the level associated with an inactive life for many hours; therefore, daily exercise will maintain your elevated metabolism and enable you to eat more without gaining weight.

*What is food to one is to others bitter poison.*

# Questions Athletes Ask about Food and Drink

Here are some questions commonly asked by athletes. You probably have similar ones, but you may also find some interesting questions you never thought of asking.

**Q.** What should I eat before a contest?

**A.** Coaches used to encourage athletes to eat a steak dinner before a game, if the athletic budget allowed it, but such pre-game meals are no longer in vogue. The fat in steak slows the digestive process, leaving food in the stomach at the beginning of the contest.

Probably your best pre-game meal, eaten about three hours before the event, contains foods familiar to your foods that agree with you, and foods that make you feel good. Avoid spicy, bulky, and high-protein foods that increase bowel and urinary activity.

**94**

Some nutritionists recommend eating the fructose sugar found in fruits, fruit juices, and honey before exercise. Unlike sucrose (table sugar), fructose is absorbed slowly from the intestine and does not stimulate the production of insulin. Since insulin reduces the sugar level in the bloodstream, lack of insulin will allow the fructose in the blood to remain there and be available for the increased energy demands during competition. A word of warning: Don't eat more than three tablespoons of honey per hour. An excess will "pull" water into the intestine and could lead to cramps, bloating, and diarrhea.

Most nutritionists say you should not eat sugar before a contest because of its tendency to stimulate the flow of insulin. On the other hand, a candy bar might provide just the energy boost you need to reach a short-term goal. Because there is still a good deal of disagreement among nutritionists, and because each individual's body chemistry is different, it may be wise to try several different but sensible pre-contest diets to see which one is most effective for you.

The pre-game meal should certainly include plenty of water so that you are fully hydrated. Even though you may drink during the game, you won't be able to replace all the fluid lost through perspiration during very active exercise.

**Q.** Is it harmful to eat sugar (sucrose)?

**A.** Sugar is pure carbohydrate and a good source of energy; however, sugar contains no other nutrients. It is better to eat other carbohydrates such as fruits, grains, and vegetables because these foods contain a variety of nutrients in addition to stored energy.

Sugar—in snacks, desserts, and on cereals—can provide some of the extra energy that a very active athlete needs. If you eat sweet foods, remember that the bacteria that cause tooth decay flourish on sugar. Thoroughly rinse your mouth and, if possible, brush your teeth after eating sweets.

**Q.** Is milk bad for athletes?

**A.** Milk is an almost perfect food, and is good for you in moderate amounts. This is not surprising since it is the only food that infants and young animals eat. There are, however, people who cannot digest lactose, the sugar found in milk. As these people grow older, they produce less lactase, the enzyme used to digest lactose, and so become increasingly unable to digest milk fully. This inability to digest milk can cause bloating, cramps, and diarrhea. If you consistently suffer from such symptoms, stop drinking milk for a week and see if your discomfort disappears. If it does, you probably do not produce sufficient lactase to digest the lactose in the milk you drink.

To obtain the nutritional value of milk, substitute yogurt and cheese where fermentation has already converted lactose to simple sugars. Or you can add Lact-Aid, which digests lactose, to your milk and continue to enjoy this healthful beverage.

**Q.** Why can some people eat and eat and never gain weight, while others get fat when they eat very little?

**A.** People's metabolism rates differ greatly. Some use amino acids efficiently in growing new cells; others do not. Some absorb digested foods readily from their intestine; others do not. To a large extent, our genetic makeup determines how we use the food we eat. Guinea pigs, like humans, require vitamin C in their diets, but rats can manufacture this vitamin from foods and can live without vitamin C in their diet. Although all humans need the same nutrients, each of us has a metabolic process that is probably as unique as our fingerprints. Incidentally, differences in our metabolic processes cause each of us to produce slightly different metabolic products. It is the differences in the odors of these products that enable a bloodhound to distinguish and follow the trail of any individual even when that trail crosses or fuses with others.

**Q.** Are mineral-containing beverages sold as "thirst quenchers" worth the price?

**A.** Probably not! In fact, if you use these drinks, it is better to dilute them with water. Otherwise, in their concentrated form, they tend to draw water into the stomach, which defeats their purpose.

Most diets supply all the minerals required to replace those lost through perspiration, so if you drink plenty of water, dehydration should not be a problem. In hot weather, when you sweat excessively during exercise, drink lots of fluid and sprinkle a little more salt on your food.

**Q.** What is carbohydrate loading?

**A.** A week before competition, an athlete entering a carbohydrate-loading procedure will exercise vigorously to exhaust the glycogen stored in his or her liver and muscles. The athlete then eats lots of protein and very few carbohydrates for three days to keep his or her body's glycogen level very low. This is followed by three days of carbohydrate loading—that is, consuming foods rich in carbohydrates in an effort to induce the body to store an excess of glycogen. These athletes believe that starving the cells of glycogen for several days will cause these same cells to store excess amounts of glycogen—much as hungry people might overeat if they were given all the food they want.

Many athletes in endurance sports, such as distance running, believe carbohydrate loading gives them a competitive edge by providing them with an excess of energy-rich glycogen at race time. But not all athletes agree.

The standard American diet has consisted of 46 percent carbohydrates, 12 percent protein, and 42 percent fats. Several years ago the Senate Select Committee on Nutrition recommended a 58–12–30 ratio for carbohydrates, proteins, and fats, thus increasing the carbohydrate portion at the expense of fats, which have been shown to be related to the buildup of plaque inside arteries. Plaque is fatty yellowish material that collects in arteries, much as lime collects in hard-water pipes, reducing the rate of blood flow and eventually clogging the artery.

The book *Food for Champions* by Ned Bayrd and Chris Quilter recommended that athletes in basic training follow a diet consisting of 68 percent carbohydrates, 12 percent proteins, and 20 percent fats. During intensive exercise a 73:12:15 ratio was recommended. In his book *Eat to Win* Dr. Robert Haas recommends a ratio of about 75:15:10. Such diets provide plenty of energy through carbohydrates. Many nutritionists now recommend that athletes, after heavy workouts, eat lots of grains and fiber instead of the initial high-protein, low-carbohydrate diet followed in traditional carbohydrate-loading programs. There is evidence that lack of carbohydrates may produce mood variations, changes in sleep patterns, and even damage to muscle tissue under stress.

Unless you're participating in vigorous contests that go on for longer than two hours, there's no point in carbohydrate loading anyway. You won't deplete your glycogen reserves in two hours.

If you want to try carbohydrate loading, talk to your coach and physician. If they approve, try it first before a practice or minor event to see if it works for you.

**Q.** Will bee pollen tablets improve my athletic performance? (The pollen actually comes from flowers that bees visit as they gather nectar.)

**A.** The price of these tablets might lead you to believe they will cure anything, but the experimental evidence is mixed. Some claim to have found an improvement in the performance of athletes taking bee pollen; others find the tablets have no effect on athletic ability or on anything else.

**Q.** Are fried foods bad for an athlete?

**A.** Fried foods are cooked in fat, and fat retards the rate at which the stomach empties; consequently, athletes should not eat fried foods before a practice or contest. To keep your fat intake at a minimum you should avoid foods fried in fat.

**Q.** To lose weight should I eliminate carbohydrates from my diet?

**A.** If you don't eat carbohydrates, your metabolic system will convert the more expensive proteins and fats to carbohydrate end products anyway. The best way to lose weight without endangering your health is to reduce, not eliminate, the intake of all kinds of food in your diet. Avoid foods rich in pure sugar, such as desserts and candy; avoid fatty foods, which provide 9 calories per gram; and avoid excess protein, too.

Generally, teenage obesity is more often the result of insufficient exercise than excess food. That's one reason athletics are so valuable for young people. Vigorous exercise will burn up the excess energy in the food that an inactive person converts to fat.

**Q.** How can I tell if I'm too fat?

**A.** One quick test is to pinch the fold of skin on the back of your arm. If it's an inch or more thick, you're probably overweight.

The table below indicates the percentage of body fat as a function of body type. Generally speaking, an athlete should have no more than 10 percent body fat, but leanness is more important for some sports than for others.

### BODY FAT AND BODY TYPE

| | | Percent Body Fat | |
|---|---|---|---|
| **Body Type** | **Condition** | **Male** | **Female** |
| Very lean | Excellent | 8–10 | 8–11 |
| Lean | Good | 11–15 | 12–16 |
| Average | Average | 16–21 | 17–23 |
| Fat | Fair | 22–25 | 24–28 |
| Very fat | Poor | 26–30 | 29–33 |
| Obese | Very poor | above 30 | above 34 |

A more accurate method is to calculate your percent body fat after measuring your waist and finding your weight. To calculate your lean body weight (LBW) use this formula:

$$LBW = (1.082 \times \text{body weight}) - (4.15 \times \text{waist [inches]}) + 98.42$$

Suppose your waist is 32 inches and you weigh 170 pounds, your LBW is 149.56 pounds:

$$LBW = (1.082 \times 170) - (4.15 \times 32) + 98.42 = 149.56 \text{ pounds}$$

The percent of your total body weight that is lean is, therefore, 88 percent because LBW/total body weight equals 149.56/170, times 100 equals 88 percent.

If your body is 88 percent lean, it must be 12 percent body fat (100 − 88 = 12).

Now measure your waist, find your weight, and calculate the percentage of your body that is fat.

The weight tables published by insurance companies may be misleading. Percent body fat is a better indicator of excess weight. An athlete might be overweight according to a weight table because of a large amount of muscle mass. Such a person might be in excellent condition and have very little body fat.

**Q.** I've tried a diet, but I can't lose weight. What should I do?

**A.** Overeating is the result of a combination of psychological factors and social customs. In one experiment, people were fed mechanically, without seeing or smelling the food, and were allowed to eat as often as they wished. Those people ate only as much as they needed. But we can't normally live under such controlled conditions.

Many hospitals and clinics throughout the country have programs that can help fat people. Before you invest in such a program, follow these tips, which might help you solve your weight problem:

- Don't eat after school or while you are watching TV. Do something else to keep busy.
- Don't eat while you read. If you have to have something in your mouth, chew sugarless gum.
- Keep a diary of everything you eat and list the calorie content next to each item.
- Eat only in the dining room or kitchen and only at mealtime.
- If your desire for food becomes overwhelming, eat some raw vegetables. Keep a supply of such food in the refrigerator for this purpose.
- When you are thirsty, drink water, not soda.
- Drink skim milk in place of whole milk.
- Don't eat desserts.
- Eat portions only half as large as those you have been eating at meals.
- Eat slowly. The hunger stimulus arises in the hypothalamus at the base of the brain. It takes about 20 minutes for satiety (fullness) sensations to reach the brain and turn off the hypothalamus. By that time a person who eats fast may already have eaten too much.
- While dieting, take a vitamin and mineral supplement to be sure you get all the nutrients you need.

**Q.** What's the truth about fats? They're an essential

nutrient; yet they are said to cause heart disease and high blood pressure.

**A.** All fats are organic compounds—that is, they consist of compounds of carbon. Fats contain three elements—carbon, oxygen, and hydrogen—and may be saturated or unsaturated. With the exception of coconut oil, all saturated fats are solids. They are called saturated because it is not possible to add any more hydrogen to the fats. Hydrogen can be taken up by (added to) unsaturated fats—a process called hydrogenation. Monounsaturated liquid fats such as olive oil, chicken fat, and peanut oil have but one (hence, "mono") carbon atom per molecule to which hydrogen can be added. Polyunsaturated liquid fats—found in corn oil, soybean oil, and fish oils—have two or more carbon atoms per molecule that will combine with hydrogen.

Saturated (animal) fats in a diet give rise to cholesterol—a chemical that tends to accumulate in, and clog, arteries in some people. Unsaturated fats do not seem to foster the formation of cholesterol.

To reduce saturated fats, and thereby cholesterol, it is good practice to avoid excess fat in your diet. Choose lean cuts of meat or eat turkey, chicken, and fish. Drink skim milk, Remove the fat that coats cold soups and gravies. Avoid cream, whipped cream, and cream cheese; they are rich in saturated fats. Use herbs and spices in place of butter to season foods, and substitute unsaturated liquid fats (oils) for the saturated fats found in vegetable shortenings, lard, and butter.

**Q.** What about foods such as pizza and hamburgers? Should athletes eat such stuff?

**A.** Actually, pizza—especially pizza with peppers and onions—provides a fairly well-balanced meal. A hamburger with lettuce, onions, tomatoes, cheese, and salad dressing provides half the daily requirement of protein, vitamin A, and niacin, one-third the daily phosphorus and calcium needs as well as more than 500 calories. But it probably contains too much fat and salt.

You should avoid candy, desserts that are rich in sugar, and snacks that are pure starch and have no nutritional value other than energy, unless you are very active.

**Q.** Can I lose weight by skipping breakfast?

**A.** You may have heard that breakfast is the most important meal of the day. Actually, it is no more essential than lunch or dinner, but it is an important meal. The time between dinner and the next morning's breakfast is the longest daily interval we have without food. Skipping breakfast will make you feel lethargic later in the morning as your blood sugar level drops. Breakfast should include some protein, as well as juice and carbohydrate, so that amino acids are available for tissue growth and repair throughout the day.

People who try to lose weight by skipping meals usually fail to do so. They are so hungry by the next meal that they eat more than they normally would.

**Q.** Are the artificial ingredients added to food dangerous?

**A.** A number of chemicals formerly added to foods are now forbidden by law. But some additives are actually beneficial. For example, vitamins and minerals are added to some foods to replace those lost in processing. Vitamin D is added to milk to prevent rickets in growing children. Calcium propionate is added to bread to retard mold growth. EDTA is used to remove tiny metal particles found in some foods. Leavening agents in bread, emulsifiers in peanut butter, and gelatin thickeners in ice cream (to prevent the growth of ice crystals) are all additives that make food tastier and more appealing. Artificial coloring is often added to enhance the appearance of food. For example, we expect butter to be yellow, but in the winter, when cows are not out to pasture, butter is nearly white unless yellow dye is added.

Sometimes additives are used because the risk is greater without them. Nitrites are known to produce cancer-causing substances in meat, but failure to use these preservatives might result in botulism, sometimes fatal food poisoning.

*. . . only the strong shall thrive;*
*. . . only the fit survive.*

# Are You in Shape?

Here are some simple tests you can use to determine your physical condition. Don't try any of these fitness indicators if you haven't been exercising or if you know you are in terrible physical condition. Instead, begin an exercise program that slowly increases your fitness. As your physical condition improves, use these tests to measure your progress.

- To test your body balance, see if you can stand on your toes with your heels together, arms extended forward, and eyes closed for 20 seconds.
- To test your power, do a standing broad jump. Can you jump a distance equal to or greater than your height?
- As a test of endurance, run in place for one minute, lifting your feet at least four inches. If you then feel out of breath and have a heart rate greater than 100 beats per minute, you do not have good endurance.
- To check your flexibility, place your legs together, lock your knees, and see if you can touch your fingers to the floor.

- Your arm strength should enable you to do 8 to 10 push-ups if you're a boy, and 6 to 8 if you're a girl.
- To test your agility, try to do 10 burpees (see Chapter 2) in 20 seconds.
- A way to test arm strength is to grasp a bathroom scale, one hand on each side, thumbs above and fingers beneath it. Squeeze the scale between your fingers and thumbs. (No fair pushing them against your legs or anything else.) The chart below will tell you how you rate in terms of arm strength.

|  | Reading on Scale (in Pounds) | |
| Arm Strength | Teenage Boys | Teenage Girls |
| --- | --- | --- |
| Excellent | 150 or more | 80 or more |
| Good | 120–150 | 60–80 |
| Fair | 90–120 | 40–60 |
| Poor | Less than 90 | Less than 40 |

- After you've been in training for a few weeks, you can try the 1½-mile run. Be sure to warm up and stretch before attempting this test. The chart below will enable you to make a rough approximation of your condition.

| | Time (in Minutes) to Run $1\frac{1}{2}$ Miles | |
| Physical Condition | Boys | Girls |
| --- | --- | --- |
| Excellent | $10\frac{1}{2}$ or less | $11\frac{1}{2}$ or less |
| Good | $10\frac{1}{2}$–$11\frac{1}{2}$ | $11\frac{1}{2}$–$12\frac{1}{2}$ |
| Average | $11\frac{1}{2}$–$13\frac{1}{2}$ | $12\frac{1}{2}$–15 |
| Fair | $13\frac{1}{2}$–16 | 15–$17\frac{1}{2}$ |
| Poor | More than 16 | More than $17\frac{1}{2}$ |

- Another test to try after you've been training awhile is the 12-minute run. How far can you run in that time?

### Distance (in Miles) run in 12 minutes

| Physical Condition | Boys | Girls |
|---|---|---|
| Excellent | More than $1\frac{3}{4}$ | More than $1\frac{2}{3}$ |
| Good | $1\frac{3}{4}$ | $1\frac{2}{3}$ |
| Average | $1\frac{1}{2}$ | $1\frac{1}{3}$ |
| Fair | $1\frac{1}{4}$ | 1 |
| Poor | 1 or less | $\frac{9}{10}$ or less |

- To test your muscular endurance have someone hold your ankles while you lie on your back with your hands folded behind your head and your knees bent. Your heels should be about 1½ feet from your buttocks. Raise your upper body so as to bring your left elbow to your right knee. Then lie back down before you raise your body again to bring your right elbow to your left knee.

  The exercise is easiest if you exhale while raising your body. Continue the exercise for exactly one minute. Have your partner watch the clock while you count the number of times you raise your body. Compare your result with this table.

### Number of Elbow-to-Knee Touches in 1 Minute

| Physical Condition | Boys | Girls |
|---|---|---|
| Excellent | More than 35 | More than 45 |
| Good | 30 – 35 | 35 – 45 |
| Average | 20 – 30 | 20 – 35 |
| Fair | 15 – 20 | 10 – 20 |
| Poor | 10 – 15 | 0 – 10 |

- The Harvard step test is another way to evaluate your general cardiovascular pulmonary (heart and lung) condition without measuring vital capacity, cardiac output, reaction time, oxygen debt, and all the other elaborate tests that might be done in a thorough medical test of your condition. In this test, you simply step up on, and down from, a bench or step at a rate of 30 times a minute for 4 minutes. The height of the bench used should depend on your height as indicated in this table.

| Height of Bench or Step | Height of Person Doing Step Test |
|---|---|
| 12″ | Less than 5′0″ |
| 14″ | 5′0″–5′3″ |
| 16″ | 5′3″–5′9″ |
| 18″ | 5′9″–6′0″ |
| 20″ | Greater than 6′0″ |

After stepping up and down from the bench 120 times in 4 minutes, wait 1 minute. Then count your heartbeats (pulse) for 30 seconds. After 2 minutes, count your heartbeats again for 30 seconds. Do the same count once more, 3 minutes after you stop exercising. From the data collected, you can calculate your recovery index according to the formula below.

$$\text{Recovery index} = \frac{\text{duration of exercise in seconds} \times 100}{\text{sum of heartbeats} \times 2}$$

Suppose you collect the following data after doing this exercise for 4 minutes (240 seconds):

| Minutes after Exercise | Count of Heartbeats |
|---|---|
| $1-1\frac{1}{2}$ | 50 |
| $2-2\frac{1}{2}$ | 45 |
| $3-3\frac{1}{2}$ | 40 |

Calculate your recovery index as follows:

$$\text{Recovery index} = \frac{240 \times 100}{(50 + 45 + 40) \times 2} = \frac{24000}{135 \times 2} \times \frac{24000}{270} = 89$$

If your score is 89, your recovery index indicates that you are in excellent condition, as the next chart shows.

| Physical Condition | Recovery Index |
|---|---|
| Poor | Less than 50 |
| Fair | 50−65 |
| Good | 65−80 |
| Excellent | Greater than 80 |

If you have difficulty finding the pulse in your wrist, put your thumb on one side of your Adam's apple and your fingers on the other side. Squeeze a little and you should feel a good pulse as your heart forces blood through the arteries in your neck.

Being in good physical condition will make you a better athlete. Even if you're not an athlete, it will make you a healthier person. You will have better circulation of blood, more red blood cells, larger lungs, a stronger heart, greater muscular strength and endurance, and a better opinion of yourself.

*Look to your health;
and if you have it,
praise God, and value it.*

# Athletics, Health, and Medicine

Our growing enthusiasm for athletics and exercise is making us healthier, but it also places us in greater danger of being injured. It's estimated that in the United States there are 17 million sport related injuries each year. Exuberant exercise has led the medical profession to create a group of sports medicine specialists called kinesiologists, who study and treat the athletes and would-be athletes who put their bodies through strenuous and sometimes debilitating motion.

Weight training can reduce injuries by increasing muscle strength; when coupled with stretching, it need not reduce flexibility. The problem has been to find the time for athletes to carry out such training and still have sufficient time for developing skills. Now there is evidence that a single set of 8 to 12 repetitions for each muscle group is sufficient provided the muscles are exercised until they fail. Since such a routine can be completed in 30 minutes, more coaches are advocating strength training twice a week during the sport season and three times a week in the off-season.

Although the initial treatment for most common athletic injuries remains the same—rest, ice, compression, and elevation (RICE)—advances in technology have provided kinesiologists and orthopedic surgeons with new tools for studying and treating athletic ills. Thin flexible light fibers that can bring light to, and images from, the interior of a joint have led to arthroscopic surgery. Instead of a 6-inch incision and exposure of a patient's entire knee joint, a tiny slit that can be covered with a Band-Aid is now often all that is needed to perform knee surgery. Recovery time is reduced from months to a few weeks, which greatly reduces the muscle atrophy that accompanies lack of use of a joint.

With transcutaneous (through-the-skin) electrical nerve stimulation (TENS), a technique that bombards sensory nerve endings to reduce pain, patients can move joints and begin muscle-strengthening exercises that speed recovery.

High-speed, high-resolution motion picture cameras enable coaches and kinesiologists to study in detail the motions of athletes and identify inefficient movements.

Cybex, a computerized machine that measures muscle strength electronically, can pinpoint weaknesses. Computers can be used to investigate various athletic techniques and conduct biomechanical analyses that enable athletes to improve their performances.

Psychologists are studying the biological clocks of individual athletes to determine when they should train in order to be at peak performance. Some people, for example, reach a physiological peak soon after they awake; others function most effectively in the afternoon or early evening. Other psychologists are trying to find, through biofeedback techniques, ways to make athletes relax, or find stimuli that create the mental state associated with the athlete's best performance.

Many professional and Olympic teams now have psychologists, computer programmers, and data analysts, as well as doctors trained in sports medicine on their staffs.

## PREVENTING ATHLETIC INJURIES

Proper warm-up and stretching before exercise, and a cool-down routine after vigorous activity, can reduce the likelihood of injury significantly.

A practical cool-down method following exercise is to reduce muscle activity gradually just as you gradually increased muscle action before you began vigorous exercise. Jogging followed by walking and stretching will cut in half the time it takes your system to remove lactic acid from tissues and will reduce muscle soreness. To replace the fluids lost during exercise, you should drink 8 to 12 ounces of water every 10 to 15 minutes until your thirst is quenched.

Common sense can reduce injuries, too. If you are tired, your reflexes will be slower and you won't be able to respond normally. This lack of muscle "memory" may precipitate injury. So get plenty of sleep. Don't try to play in games or participate in hard workouts if you're tired. Similarly, don't aggravate an injury by trying to play through pain. Pain is nature's way of telling you to stop whatever is causing the pain.

Finally, don't roughhouse or let others roughhouse. Injuries often occur on the field or court. Some of these are inevitable. Locker-room, classroom, and shower-room injuries, however, are totally unnecessary. They give coaches gray hair and teams poor records.

Knowledge and common sense can help to ensure good health. Brushing your teeth after meals is a way of getting rid of food caught between your teeth. The sugar in these foods is quickly changed to acids by bacteria in your mouth. These acids attack the enamel that covers your teeth causing tooth decay.

Tooth damage has been greatly reduced in contact sports by requiring participants to wear mouth guards. Be sure you wear yours during practices as well as during games.

Avoid exposing your ears to loud noises. They can reduce your hearing. You may enjoy rock music, but enjoy it at a moderate volume. Many young people are partly deaf as a result of listening to heavily amplified music.

Acne is a common skin disorder among teenagers. It is believed to be caused by the hormone testosterone, which stimulates skin glands to secrete an oily substance that blocks the skin follicles. Bacteria may act on these oily deposits, causing inflammation. Squeezing these pimples merely spreads the infection and can create scars, so don't squeeze them. See a dermatologist who can prescribe cleansing agents, bactericides, and, if necessary, antibiotics.

Avoid extensive exposure to the sun, especially during the midday hours. If you must be in the sun, use sun-screen lotions. The sun can cause severe burns, and prolonged exposure may lead to skin cancer.

Your eyes can be damaged by too much or too little

light. Wear sunglasses or a cap with a visor in bright sunlight and never look directly at the sun. Reading in dim light can cause eyestrain. Always read or study with plenty of light on the subject.

If you get a speck in your eye, it can usually be washed away with tears. Pull your upper eyelid out and over the lower one. If that doesn't work, cover your eye with some protective material—a gauze pad will do—and seek medical help.

If you have asthma, keep a bronchodilator available during practices and games. Be sure to alert your coaches to the fact that you are asthmatic.

Do not use alcohol, marijuana, tobacco in any form, or other drugs.

If you have weak ankles, wear ankle wraps when you exercise. Some coaches insist that all players use such support. Very weak ankles should be taped. High-top sneakers will also reduce ankle sprains if fully and properly laced.

## TESTS FOR ABNORMALITIES

Stand in front of a full-length mirror wearing only shorts. Your kneecaps should both be directed straight ahead. If one turns inward or outward, you have an abnormality (femoral torsion) that may make you susceptible to leg injuries. Or are you bowlegged, knock-kneed, or pigeon-toed? Look at your toes. Is the second toe longer than the big toe? Such a condition is known as Morton's foot and often causes leg problems for athletes who run a lot.

Some people have adapted to these abnormal structures so that they experience no diffficulty. It is certainly not unusual to see a bowlegged or pigeon-toed baseball player. But if you do have one of these abnormalities and are experiencing foot or leg problems, see a podiatrist or a doctor who specializes in sports medicine.

## SOME COMMON ATHLETIC INJURIES AND PROBLEMS

### The "blahs"

If you feel tired, your muscles are sore, you've lost your appetite, you're thirsty all the time, you're irritable and lack enthusiasm and confidence, you probably have the "blahs." These subjective signs can be confirmed by such objective indicators as an elevated heart rate while at rest, a decline in athletic performance, a weight loss of several pounds, difficulty breathing at a slower athletic pace than normal, changes in your normal bowel-movement pattern, and difficulty sleeping.

The blahs are a result of too much training. You need to rest or reduce your level of exercise. Perhaps you're training hard every day when you might make greater progress by training every other day with light workouts in between. Or perhaps you've been practicing without enough sleep. Although individuals vary in their need for sleep, most need from six to ten hours. Determine how many hours you need and get them every night.

### Heat Exhaustion

Vigorous exercise in hot, humid weather can lead to heat exhaustion or heat stroke, particularly in the early season if an athlete is not in good physical condition.

The symptoms of heat exhaustion are profuse perspiration changing to a cold, clammy sweat, nausea, headache, dizziness, a faint feeling, shallow breathing, a weak, rapid pulse, and possibly a pale face.

Lay the athlete on his or her back, out of the sun, feet elevated to reduce the fainting sensation. Remove excess clothing and sponge the body with cold water or ice packs. Later, have the athlete shower in lukewarm water.

Heat stroke is even more serious. The athlete stops sweating, the skin is hot and dry, body temperature may rise to 106°F or higher. He or she may complain of burning sensations in the legs and chest, breathing difficulty, nausea, chest pains, and headache, and may even lose consciousness.

Wrap the patient in cold, wet sheets or other cloth, or get him or her under a cold shower (if conscious) or into a cold bath. Get a doctor to the scene or take the athlete—wrapped in cold, wet cloth—to a doctor or an emergency room.

To avoid ill effects from workouts in hot weather, athletes should prepare for practice in the heat through pre-season training under such conditions. Such training, done gradually, will improve circulation to the skin, reduce salt loss from the kidneys, and increase the sweating mechanism's capacity to shed excess body heat.

You can reduce the likelihood of succumbing to the heat by drinking plenty of fluid before, during, and after practice. You should get to a cooler place and sit down if you feel nauseated, dizzy, or cold, or if you experience any other abnormal symptoms. Don't risk a bout with heat stroke. Remember, you can make only one fatal mistake!

### Frostbite

Skiers, hikers, and year-round runners should not stay outside for long periods if the wind-chill factor is lower than 10° below zero F. Serious frostbite can occur in cold weather. Be sure your face, ears, hands, and feet, as well as the rest of your body, are well covered. Should you find signs of frostbite, such as cold, whitish areas of skin, soak them in water at about body temperature (100°F). Don't massage. Don't rub with snow. Do seek medical treatment.

### Pain in Side

Exercise often causes a stitch, or pain in the side. Usually the stitch is in the right side. It is caused by a muscular spasm of the diaphragm, which separates the chest and abdominal cavities. Its cause varies—response to an oxygen debt, faulty breathing, a weak diaphragm, unusual stretching, and so forth. If it bothers you frequently, try to breathe regularly and deeply and stretch your midbody thoroughly before exercising.

### Bloody Urine

An exhausting workout will sometimes result in some blood being passed in the urine. If it persists, or if it is extensive, you should seek medical help.

### Muscle Cramps

Cramps may occur when muscles are tired, overstretched, bruised, or deficient in salt or other minerals. Relief usually can be obtained by mildly stretching the muscle with simultaneous rubbing. Warmth can help, too. Some trainers believe the incidence of cramps can be reduced if athletes take vitamin C and drink a cool salt solution (1 tablespoon salt in a gallon of water) following practice.

### Blisters

Blisters are caused by friction. Sometimes ill-fitting shoes are the cause, or a sock may slide back and forth over skin. Be sure your shoes fit. If they are new, wear them for short periods of time until they are broken in. Wearing two pairs of socks may prevent blisters. When you feel friction, stop and cover the area with a pad, or change your shoes.

Blisters can be treated effectively by a trainer, nurse, or doctor.

### Nosebleed

Place a cold pack over your nose. If bleeding continues, hold the nostrils firmly between your thumb and forefinger until clotting occurs. Spit out blood that flows into your throat. Should your nose appear to be broken, or should bleeding persist, seek medical attention.

### Blow to the Testes

This painful injury can be treated by placing the athlete on his back, loosening his belt, and pushing his knees gently to his chest a few times. Usually the pain will disappear in a few minutes. If it does not, he should see a physician.

### Bruise

A blow to the body can cause bleeding beneath the skin, followed by swelling. To treat the bruise, or contusion, apply ice or cold compresses to reduce bleeding, elevate the body part, and apply a compression bandage. Heat treatment or whirlpool will help *after* the swelling disappears. If the area is sore, the player should have the bruise padded before entering competition.

### Breast Bruise

Treat like any other contusion. Examine for any nodules after the injury improves or if pain persists. The likelihood of such an injury can be reduced by wearing a sports bra.

### Charley horse

A charley horse, or hematoma, is a severe bruise that causes bleeding within muscle tissue. It is characterized by tenderness, swelling, inability to run, and possible muscle spasms. Treat as you would a bruise, with plenty of ice, compression, and elevation. If possible, stretch the muscle immediately after the injury to prevent muscle spasms and to reduce bleeding.

Unless the injury is severe, activity—after the swelling subsides—will aid in removing blood from the hematoma.

### Athlete's Foot

Athlete's foot is a fungal infection that causes an itching, burning sensation. It can be treated with an antifungal cream, ointment, or powder.

To prevent this infection, wear dry socks and shoes, use an antifungal powder in your shoes and socks, dry thoroughly between your toes after showering, and wear sandals in the locker room. Don't walk around in your bare feet.

### Bone Bruise or Stone Bruise

This kind of bruise is usually caused by stepping on a stone while running or by landing on your heel after a jump. Treat it by applying ice. Also, wear cushioned insoles in your shoes as long as pain is present.

### Sprains

Sprains result from damage to the ligaments that form bands across the joints. Sprains vary in severity. In severe sprains, ligaments are torn off the bone; in mild ones, a few fibers are stretched.

Many sprains of the ankle can be prevented by wearing proper footwear, not running on uneven surfaces, wearing ankle wraps, or taping a weak ankle.

Apply ice or cold compresses, or soak in ice water immediately. If, after five minutes, you cannot walk or bear full weight on your leg, you should not exercise further. Continue treating with ice, compression, and elevation. Don't walk on the leg until medical advice is available. X-rays may be necessary to see if there is a break or a severe sprain.

### Strains

A strain involves damage to tendon and/or muscle tissue. It is the result of too much stress on or overuse of muscles. Many strains would never occur if muscles were warmed up and stretched before exercise.

Apply ice and compression to the injury. Once the swelling is down, you can apply moist heat. Generally, strains require rest. An athlete should not attempt to play until all pain is gone. Mild exercise and stretching to the point of pain are permissible.

A hamstring strain is usually accompanied by a

sharp, snapping sensation with severe pain. After treating, strengthening exercises should begin only after muscles can be thoroughly stretched.

Groin strains, which prevent an athlete from running fast, jumping, or twisting, appear less suddenly than hamstring pulls, but the causes are similar.

After applying ice and compression, and resting for several days, you may benefit from whirlpool treatments and mild exercise with elastic bandage support in the form of a figure eight from the groin, around your leg, then around your waist and back to the groin.

Shin splints are strains of the soleus and tibialis muscles, or their tendons, on the front of the leg—a leg that may feel as though it's on fire. Often the shinbone will feel sandpapery when you run your hand along it. This is the result of many small ruptures in these lower leg muscles.

Shin splints have many causes. These include running on very hard (concrete) or very soft (sand) surfaces, running in spiked shoes, running too long on the toes, weak arches, or attempting strenuous training too soon.

The best cure is complete rest and moist heat.

To avoid shin splints, stay away from the causes listed above, do some backward running, don't always run in the same direction on a track or road, and do plenty of stretching and strengthening exercises for the anterior muscles of the lower leg.

Stretch the shin muscles by turning your toes as far forward as you can while seated on the floor or by having someone pull your toes forward.

To strengthen the shin muscles, do exercise 6 (Chapter 3).

Exercise without proper warm-up and stretching, up-hill or downhill running, sprints before legs are properly conditioned, a tight calf muscle, or a naturally short Achilles tendon may cause this tendon to tear, producing swelling, pain, and inflammation.

This tendon is slow to heal, but proper stretching, a heel lift in shoes, and heat before exercise followed by rubbing the tendon with ice for ten minutes after cool-down may enable you to continue exercising. Of course, severe tears or ruptures of this tendon will make movement impossible and may require surgery.

Tennis elbow or pitcher's elbow causes pain when the athlete tries to lift his or her forearm with the palm of the hand turned down. This strain may result from forces placed on the tendons near the elbow by the large muscles of the arm when the player turns the wrist and forearm swinging a racquet or when throwing balls, especially curve balls.

Sometimes heat and rest will provide relief, but young pitchers should not throw for long periods of time or attempt to throw curve balls or screwballs.

### Knee Problems

The knee was not made to twist or turn with the entire body's weight on it, but this happens in some sports, especially contact sports where additional forces may be placed on the knee. Torn ligaments and cartilage are common knee injuries that require the attention of an orthopedist.

Some knee problems arise from overuse rather than trauma (injury). Chondromalacia, for example, is an irritation of the underside of the kneecap (patella). Overuse may cause the kneecap to get out of alignment and rub against bone rather than cartilage. This causes pronounced pain after sitting or when climbing stairs. Often the knee will feel stiff in the morning. While running, especially downhill, it may feel as though the kneecap is slipping out of position. There may also be grinding sounds when the leg is extended.

As with most injuries, temporary relief may be achieved with ice, rest, elevation, and aspirin to reduce swelling. Often, knee disorders due to overuse are caused by wearing poorly fitting athletic shoes or by abnormal leg anatomy. Better shoes, inserts prescribed by a competent podiatrist or sports medicine specialist, together with exercises to strengthen the quadriceps and stretch the hamstrings, can often eliminate the difficulty.

Many athletes simply work too hard. An extensive, exhaustive workout is valuable a couple of times each week, but not every day. Constant overwork can produce tendonitis in any of the various tendons around the knee. Treatment similar to that used for chondromalacia will help relieve the symptoms and may provide a cure.

### Lower Back Problems

A twisting fall, improper lifting or bending, or sleeping in a soft bed can produce pain and muscle spasms in the lower back (sacroiliac area) that will prevent you from bending your trunk or fully flexing one leg while lying on your back.

Usually the disorder can be cured by sleeping on a bed with a sheet of plywood under the mattress, whirlpool treatment, the special back-stretching exercises in Chapter 2, and the strengthening exercises for *both back* and *abdominal* muscles (antagonists) described in Chapter 3. To relieve the severe pain, which must be accomplished before exercise begins, a physician may have to prescribe muscle relaxants.

If the pain is the result of differences in leg length (not uncommon) or lack of spinal alignment, shoe inserts or special shoes may be required.

### Potentially Very Serious Injuries

Dislocations, broken bones, and serious neck, head, and back injuries should always be attended to by a doctor. Make no attempt to move people with possible injuries to the central nervous system (brain and spine).

### Exercise When Injured

If rest seems essential to recovering from an injury, you may be concerned that all your training has been for nothing. Without exercise you will not be physically fit when you are finally healed. After talking with your physician, you may find that you can swim or cycle despite your injury. If that's true, you can maintain your fitness program as you recover. One mile of swimming provides as much exercise as four miles of running; four miles of cycling is equivalent to a mile of running.

### More Information

If you would like more information about sports medicine, write to one or all of the following:

- American Academy of Osteopathic Sports Medicine
  c/o Osteopathic Medicine
  Suite 2080
  1603 Orrington Avenue
  Evanston, Illinois 60201

- American Academy of Podiatric Sports Medicine
  c/o American Podiatry Association
  20 Chevy Chase Circle
  Washington, DC 20015

- American Orthopedic Society for Sports Medicine
  Suite 202
  70 West Hubbard Street
  Chicago, Illinois 60610

## DRUGS AND SPORTS

For years, coaches have warned athletes not to smoke or drink. Now coaches warn players not to smoke, drink, or do drugs. Are coaches right in asking, even insisting, that their athletes refrain from using cigarettes, beer, marijuana, cocaine, steroids and other drugs?

The overwhelming evidence that cigarettes cause heart disease, emphysema, and cancer, especially lung cancer led the government to require that all cigarette packages carry a warning from the surgeon general. There can be no doubt that alcoholism adversely affects the lives of millions. Alcoholics, unable to do their jobs, are fired; their families suffer, and the killings by drunks who attempt to drive are well known to all who read a daily newspaper. Newspapers recount, as well, the constant battles between law-enforcement agencies and those who sell and promote the sales of such illegal substances as marijuana, cocaine, heroin, LSD, MDA, PCP, and other drugs.

Unquestionably long-term effects of smoking, drinking, and drugs are devastating. But what about the short-term effects of these substances? Can a couple of drinks, cigarettes, or joints have any harmful effects on an athlete's performance?

## Smoking

The long-term effects of the nicotine and tars in cigarettes cause serious health problems. Unfortunately, those who start smoking find it very hard to stop. "I wish I had never started smoking" is a sentence commonly used by adult smokers.

A young athlete's life is not threatened by a couple of cigarettes, but his or her athletic performance is. Smoke from cigarettes coats the linings of the lungs, reducing the amount of oxygen that can be transferred to an athlete's blood and eventually to his or her muscles. Thus, athletes who smoke even a small amount have less endurance than they would have if they did not smoke.

## Marijuana

The smoke from marijuana, like that from cigarettes, reduces the body's ability to transfer oxygen.

In some people, marijuana alters the perception of time and space and provides a pleasant euphoria. Frequently, it gives a person unwarranted confidence despite loss of muscle coordination and eye-tracking ability that makes driving after pot smoking as dangerous as after drinking. In tests conducted on people who were high on marijuana, many of the subjects reported that they felt the drawings or writing they were asked to do were the best they had ever done. When shown their art or writing on the following day, they were shocked by the poor quality of what they had actually drawn or written.

Alcohol has similar effects, but alcohol is water soluble. Within a few hours, most of the alcohol a person consumes has been oxidized, releasing its 7.5 calories per gram. Most of the two thousand or more chemicals in marijuana smoke, include THC (delta-9-tetrahydrocannabinol) are fat soluble. They collect in the fatty tissue of the brain, adrenals, gonads, and elsewhere, and leave the body very slowly. In fact, the half-life of cannabinoids is about a week; that is, it takes about a week to rid the body of half the cannabinoids taken in at any one time.

In addition to marijuana's tendency to alter one's sense of time and space, and to reduce muscle coordination, the drug has serious psychological effects. It causes both short-term and long-term memory loss and leads to reduced motivation and ambition—traits commonly associated with "potheads"—or the "amotivational syndrome," as it is known among psychologists.

Among heavy or longtime male users of marijuana, the drug is known to cause abnormal sperm cells, reduce the sperm count, increase the number of cells with missing chromosomes, decrease the rate of cell division, disrupt the movement of chromosomes, and lower testosterone (male sex hormone) production. Female users may cease to ovulate because of changes in the female sex hormones that regulate the menstrual cycle.

While controlled experimentation with teenagers is not possible, we do know that those who smoke marijuana regularly have abnormal, immature brain-wave patterns as seen on electroencephalographs (EEGs). About three months after these people stop using the drug, their brain waves return to normal. In rhesus monkeys, where controlled research with marijuana has been done, abnormal brain waves, seen on EEGs, are associated with changes in brain cells and indications of nerve cell deterioration. In female monkeys, there were nearly four times as many terminations of pregnancy (miscarriages) in animals using marijuana as there were in normal non-smoking females.

Human users are plagued by an increase in the enzymes that digest lung tissue, and a reduction of as much as 25 percent in air flow to the lungs. The condensates (liquids) formed when marijuana and tobacco smoke cool are carcinogenic (cancer-causing) and readily produce cancerous growths when spread on the skin of mice.

Generally, the signs of marijuana use among teenagers are a chronic cough and chest pains. People close to young users of pot or other drugs may notice a change in the user's life-style and personal appearance, as well as periodic losses of memory, confused states of mind, a tendency to be more isolated, more frequent temper outbursts, and, at times, an unwarranted sense of confidence. In addition, they may notice that the person has drowsy spells, is often hungry, associates with known drug users, has secretive phone calls, wears sunglasses (to hide red eyes) at odd times, tends to be more secretive and suspicious of others, and may have spoons, rubber tubing, syringes, eyedroppers, or needles in his or her room.

If you have a teammate or a friend who has symptoms that convince you he or she is drinking or "doing drugs," you should point out that you are concerned. Offer to help, But try not to confront your friend while he or she is under the influence of the drug. You may be more successful than adults. Often users refuse to face the facts about pot when confronted. They are un-willing to admit that they have undergone changes while on the drug. If possible, get your friend to talk to his or her parent or guardian about the problem.

## Alcohol

Alcohol, by itself, is a depressant. Initially, it reduces inhibitions and makes socializing easier; however, it also reduces one's ability to reason logically and to think things through. This water-soluble drug is quickly absorbed from the stomach into the blood stream. It dehydrates the body which carries away vi-tal minerals. Its effect on the nervous system causes loss of coordinated movements and a lack of concern and caution that can lead to automobile accidents and other mishaps. Driving while intoxicated is a major cause of fatal accidents in this country. For your own sake, never ride in a car driven by someone who has been drinking.

Although dangerous in its own right, alcohol, when combined with other substances, can be lethal. A combination of alcohol and phenobarbitol can cause death. Alcohol combined with aspirin can cause stom-ach and intestinal bleeding. It reduces the effective-ness of antidiabetic drugs such as tolbutamide as well as antibiotics and anticoagulants.

There are numerous reports of youths who, in an ef-fort to draw attention to themselves, drank a quart of whiskey and soon stopped breathing. Make no mis-take about it, alcohol is dangerous!

## Steriods

In 1983, American athletes left the Pan-American Games because they feared tests would reveal that they had been taking steroids—a practice forbidden in Olympic and other major meets.

Some teenagers have tried to purchase steroids because such drugs are said to increase strength by stimulating muscle growth.

Steroids are an artificial facsimile of testosterone, a male sex hormone. They are sometimes prescribed for old people and postoperative patients because they cause rapid assimilation of protein and, therefore, build muscle tissue.

Steroids are forbidden in some sports (and probably should be forbidden in all sports) because they are an artificial stimulant with very dangerous side effects. The football player taking steroids may be bigger and stronger than before, but he's also meaner, more hostile, more impatient, and harder to live with. Steroids can provide muscle strength that exceeds the tear limits of tendons and ligaments. One weight lifter, in jerking a huge weight, tore his kneecap from its tendons.

Despite the great damage involved in taking steroids, more than half of the one hundred athletes polled by a doctor said they would take the drug, knowing it might kill them in a year, if it would make them Olympic champions. Dedication to athletics is fine, but such an obsession is just plain idiotic.

### Blood Boosting

It is clear that taking steroids to increase one's strength is an artificial and dangerous method that should be forbidden. But what about blood boosting using one's own blood? A month or so before an event, an athlete has a quart of blood removed from his or her body. The plasma portion of the blood is returned to the body, but the red blood cells are separated from the plasma, frozen, and stored. Then, shortly before a contest, the cells are reinjected into the athlete's bloodstream, giving a blood boost. Results of this technique show that an athlete's stamina may be increased by one-third a day after the red blood cells are added to the blood. Some effect is still evident and felt a week later. Not only stamina, but speed as well may improve.

Should such a technique be approved? In one sense, it's a form of cheating; yet no artificial chemicals are involved. Unless blood counts are taken frequently, it would be hard to detect the athlete who received a blood boost.

## DRUGS AND IMMATURITY

Often young people get into drugs (alcohol is a drug, too) because they lack self-confidence or social skills. Drugs give them a false confidence that causes them to continue to use the drugs. They feel more secure within; yet, to others, these young people may seem strange, even foolish. Their behavior appears immature, and they can't cope with life's normal problems. Their grades decline, their athletic performances fall off, their behavior patterns change, and they begin to choose drug-addicted people as their friends.

A boy or girl actively and successfully engaged in sports usually has enough self-confidence so that he or she does not need the artificial confidence that drugs instill. But for those who do not find success or enjoyment in a particular sport, the temptation and pressure to find false happiness is greater. For these people, it is probably best to find another sport that is more suited to their skills. Or, for various reasons, it may be that athletics are simply not right for them. These people should find some type of exercise they enjoy in order to remain physically fit, but they should find another interest where they can achieve success. It may be in drama, singing, dancing, civic service, hospital work, writing, working with animals, or academic pursuits. The point is, find something you enjoy, something that makes you feel good inside and pursue it. Don't give up on the positive side of life and search for false pleasures that ultimately can bring only unhappiness.

Problems are a part of life. They are best solved by rational, thoughtful consideration and, sometimes, discussion. Solutions cannot be found by a mind clouded with substances unnatural to the human body. Attempts to avoid problems through drugs can only delay the process of maturation. No society wants to contend with twenty-year-olds who lack the maturity to face and handle the daily problems that life brings.

*For 'tis the mind that makes the
body rich.*

# Get Psyched

A weak team sometimes upsets a team that is vastly superior physically. How can this happen? The answer, of course, is that the mental aspect of athletics is just as important as the physical. An unbeaten team may feel complacent as they approach a game with a team known to be weaker. The poorly rated team, on the other hand, feeling they have nothing to lose and smarting from defeats, may suddenly develop pride, determination, and a will to win that more than compensate for inferior physical ability or size.

The mental state most appropriate for a sport varies with the sport. A baseball or softball player must be relaxed. Tenseness will only impair the fine, smooth motor coordination so essential to the game. Football, however, is, according to many coaches, at least 50 percent psychological. A player who isn't "up" for the game is not going to play at maximum potential.

The growing role of psychologists in the training of

professional and Olympic teams certainly indicates
that coaches, managers, and owners recognize that the
mind is as vital to athletics as the body.

## QUALITIES OF A WINNER

We know that an athlete needs physical skills; however, these qualities alone do not make a winner. To
win, an athlete must be in the right frame of mind.

If you fear failure, you will probably fail. So think
positively and strive for perfection, even though you
realize that perfection is impossible. Do your best by
setting realistic goals, recognizing that there will be
setbacks along the way.

An athlete must be aggressive, but the aggression
must be controlled. A winner will play hard, but will
not lose control and become a "killer" bent on winning at any cost. The desire to win should be evident,
but it should be governed by sensitivity and confidence that allow for graceful losing. There is no shame
in losing when you have done your best to win. Nor
should anxiety about winning make you a nervous
wreck with sweaty palms, shaky knees, and nausea.

A winner learns from defeat. He or she focuses on
flaws and strives to correct them by devoting practice
time to overcoming weaknesses and enhancing
strengths. A winner is willing to take risks, to compete with other winners, knowing that good competition is the only way to test limits and potentials—
potentials that should not be underestimated. Before
1954, the 4-minute mile was believed to be a goal that
no runner could attain. Then Roger Bannister ran the

mile in less than 4 minutes. After his achievement became known, ten other runners mastered the feat within two years.

Finally, winners do not overtrain. They recognize that athletics are a part of life, not life itself, and that an excess of athletic training can bring physical deterioration and mental staleness. The serious athlete who doesn't enjoy his or her sport, or can't attain the physical and mental balance that provides a winning edge, will feel the frustration of losing. A good coach or parent can help the athlete who needs to establish a better balance; the athlete who dislikes a sport should drop it and find another sport or activity that is enjoyable and rewarding.

## KNOW YOURSELF

Everyone has two selves. There is the first or active self that others see; the self that consists of the actions we take in response to stimuli. It functions through senses, nerves, brain centers, and muscles. The second self is judgmental. It involves the more subtle thought and verbal facets of the active brain. It assesses what you do, forms opinions, often critical, of your other self's performance, and conceptualizes.

The successful athlete is able to silence the second self during athletic activity and concentrate on actions without making assessments or judging the performance. The first self focuses only on the present, on what is, on the smooth, rhythmic muscular contractions that athletics require. The first self enables us to carry out routine, learned motions easily, without thinking. We walk, run, eat, ride a bike, tie our shoes, brush our teeth, throw a ball, and do a vast number of things without having to think about what we're doing.

It's the second self that gives athletes trouble, that prevents the baseball or tennis player from concentrating on the ball and seeing the ball meet the bat or racquet. The second self may be concerned not with what *is* happening but what *will* happen. By diverting the athlete's attention to concerns about winning, past failures, self-image, and the opponent's successes or skills, the second self interferes with the first self's routine behavior, raising doubts that are often self-fulfilling and breaking the athlete's concentration on the here and now.

During athletic action the second self should be shut out; the athlete should concentrate on watching the ball, the puck, the opponent, or the track or path just ahead. There is a time for the second self, but not during a contest.

The second self is useful when it's time to assess your ability as an athlete objectively and realistically, to ask certain questions: Do I have the qualifications for the sport in terms of size, stamina, speed, strength, and coordination? If not, can I overcome my difficulties? What are my strengths? What are my weaknesses? Why am I competing—for the enjoyment? For social reasons? In order to relax? To develop physical fitness? What must I do to improve? Do I have the time to become really good at this sport? Do I want to be really good?

If films of your performances are available, watch them with a coach, parent, or a competent older competitor in the sport. Break the sport into its component skills. Evaluate your ability in each skill with help from an older person. Decide what you need to do to improve your skills in the sport. You may even find that you're better suited for a different sport. Whether you want to change sports will probably depend on your attitude toward your present sport and the proposed sport. If you thoroughly enjoy the sport you're in, you'll probably want to stick with it even if you may never set any records.

You may find, particularly in team sports, that your position or role on the team is not the one you would have chosen. Try to look at your role on the team from your coach's frame of reference. He or she may be playing you at a particular position because you have skills that no one else on the team possesses. Or the position you'd like may be held by an athlete with skills superior to yours, at least in that position.

If, after you've considered the situation carefully, you think you'd be of greater service to the team in another position, talk to your coach in private. Present your case objectively and politely. Listen to the coach's response and abide by his or her decision.

Above all, remember that a coach isn't critical of your play because he or she doesn't like you. A coach or instructor looks for errors or weaknesses in your game in order to help you correct them. Cooperate by concentrating, listening, asking questions, and working hard to learn from your mistakes.

## PSYCH-OUTS

Some opponents you will encounter are naturals at performing the psych-out. They may not play very well, but they've learned, either by design or by accident, that they can gain an edge by upsetting your composure. Again, concentration will make you oblivious to the psych-out artist, but in case you slip, be aware of such psych-out techniques as distraction, air of superiority, guilt feelings, intimidation, taunting, and the cold shoulder.

Distraction is the method used by a catcher who talks to all the hitters in an effort to break their concentration and take their mind off the ball. A more violent form is the temper tantrum or the antics performed by some tennis players who are essentially saying, "I'm the center of attraction. You're nobody."

The superiority method is designed to make you feel that you're inferior. Your opponent might say, "Too bad you missed that shot. You had the right idea. I used to have the same problem until I learned how to meet the ball a bit earlier. Maybe I can help you after the match."

Or you may get the cold shoulder before and during a contest. This approach is designed to make you feel that you're nothing. The match is a mere formality that must be played to satisfy league rules.

Inducing feelings of guilt is a technique used by some inferior players. They may say, "Wow, you're really good." or "Gee, you're outstanding! We don't really belong on the same field. I'm sorry to be such poor competition." This technique seeks to make you think, at least subconsciously, "How can I beat such a nice person?" Then, when you relax and decide to take it easy on your poor overmatched opponent, he or she suddenly rallies and wins because you lost your enthusiasm for winning.

Some players try to dominate by intimidation. They'll shout and roar and threaten, hoping to make you feel you can never match such aggressive "play."

Taunting, or teasing among very young players, is a technique that may lead you to respond to the ridicule by becoming angry and losing your concentration.

## AVOIDING PSYCH-OUTS

The best way to avoid being psyched out is to concentrate, relax, and play your game, not your opponent's game. Of course, this is easier said than done.

You must learn to avoid anger by identifying its cause. For example, are you angry because your teammates don't give their all? If so, encourage them to do better. Vent your frustration in a positive way. Talk to yourself if it helps you to concentrate. Use the relaxation techniques discussed below. Think positively; shut out that second self while you play.

Look for your opponent's weaknesses. Can he only drive to the right? Is her backhand weak? Is his pass defense weaker on one side than the other? Ask for a time out, or find a way to delay the contest if your opponent has enjoyed a string of successes.

Psych-out techniques are designed to make an opponent "choke." "Choking" is the word athletes use to describe a competitor who allows self-doubt to take over, who allows the second self to subdue the first self. The internal signs of choking are a feeling of panic, a rapidly thumping heart accompanied by tight muscles that inhibit coordinated movement, cold wet palms, constricted bronchial tubes that lead to shortness of breath, blurred vision, and an inability to concentrate. The choke is initiated when panic or anxiety causes the pituitary gland to stimulate excessive secretion of adrenaline from the adrenal glands.

## RELAXATION TECHNIQUES

To prevent choking and maintain concentration through an active first self, you may benefit from learning how to relax before and during athletic contests. Some athletes find it easy to relax and concentrate on the action in their sport, but most can benefit from relaxation techniques.

Dr. Herbert Benson is among many who believe we can learn to concentrate by sitting quietly in a comfortable place and repeating the same key word (a word such as "ball" or "puck") while trying not to think. The idea is to learn to screen out the second self even while the first self is inactive. After a number of such sessions, the length of concentration time can be gradually reduced. Ultimately, just saying the key word will provide complete concentration. Some find it helpful to hold a ball or other object as they focus their complete attention on the object and repeat the key word.

One relaxation technique is to tense each of the body's major muscle groups, in turn, for a period of 30 seconds. The muscles are then relaxed as you say, "Relax." After some time, the word "relax" is so strongly associated with relaxed muscles that merely saying the word is enough to bring about relaxation. An athlete who has learned this technique simply says the word "relax" when he or she feels muscle tension or choke sensations. A modification of this technique is to tense and then relax all major muscles at increasing levels of tension. The process is done for 15 minutes, twice a day. After a while, a few deep breaths followed by tensing and relaxing a few muscles will enable the entire body to relax.

Before a contest some find it beneficial to tense each major muscle group for just 5 seconds and then let the muscles relax while breathing evenly and deeply using the diaphragm. Often, a deep breath is all that is needed to relax muscles during an athletic event.

All these methods are modifications of yoga, a Hindu discipline that seeks to achieve control of body and mind through exercises and concentration techniques.

Many athletes improve both their skills and their confidence through mental practice—a technique that Dr. Richard Suinn calls visuo-motor behavior rehearsal (VMBR). The athlete visualizes a particular set of muscle actions involved in a skill. A tennis player "sees" the perfect serve; a baseball player sees the ball go off the bat. Jack Nicklaus always pictures a shot in his mind before he actually makes it. He can see, in slow motion, the club meeting the ball. His eye is on the ball, and his left arm is straight; he visualizes the follow-through as his concentration remains fixed on the ball's former position. Steve Hegg would practice a downhill ski run in his head the night before the event.

Most psychologists believe that mental rehearsals can improve an athletic skill. Once you learn to relax and concentrate, mental rehearsals will help you perfect a skill. Photographs of the action at various points in the motion, TV images of an outstanding athlete's performance that have been etched in your mind, or even a vivid description of the skill can serve as a model for you to focus on. With your eyes closed, imagine the action in slow motion. Note how each part of the body moves in harmony. Repeat the process several times. Check your images against photographs, film, videotape, or live television. Once you're happy with your mental images, repeat the mental rehearsal at normal speed.

Subconsciously, mental rehearsals will send nerve impulses to appropriate muscles. You can actually practice with your eyes closed and your body relaxed. Try it! See if you don't agree that it helps.

When you actually practice the skill, do it at half-speed, eyes closed, until you feel it is correct in all details. Then do it with your eyes open. Next, try it at normal speed, eyes open. Then, if it's not dangerous to do so, repeat with your eyes closed. "Freeze" your motion at various points in the action. Check the positions of your arms, legs, head, and body when "frozen." Do they agree with your mental images?

Experiments have shown that basketball players who practice shooting while blindfolded and then with their eyes open, improve their shooting more quickly than those who always practice with eyes open. Shooting without seeing seems somehow to provide better muscle sense.

When you think about your play, try to recall and visualize the good parts of your game; forget the bad plays you made. Visualizing your bad moves will only reinforce them. It's the good aspects of your game that you want to reinforce and ingrain in your nervous system.

If you have trouble relaxing and concentrating and so can't screen out your second self, you may need a concentrated program that will enable you to develop a more positive self-image and let your first self shine through.

*Sports Psyching* by Tutko and Tosi (see the Bibliography) contains a six-week program that might prove useful. A book on yoga or a series of yoga classes may help you if you can devote the time to such a program.

Whether you win or lose—and everyone does both—it's just a matter of degree. Remember Grantland Rice's immortal words:

> When the One Great Scorer comes to write against
> your name—He marks—not that you won or
> lost—but how you played the game.

# Bibliography

Anderson, Bob. *Stretching*. Bolinas, CA: Shelter Publications, Inc., 1980.

Blide, Richard Rylander. *7 Steps to Heart and Lung Fitness*. Winter Park, FL: Anna Publishing Inc., 1978.

Darden, Ellington. *Conditioning for Football*. Winter Park, FL: Anna Publishing Inc., 1979.

_____. *How Your Muscles Work*. Winter Park, FL: Anna Publishing, Inc., 1978.

_____. *Nutrition for Athletes*. Winter Park, FL: Anna Publishing, Inc., 1978.

_____. *Olympic Athletes Ask Questions about Exercise and Nutrition*. Winter Park, FL: Anna Publishing, Inc., 1977.

_____. *Strength Training Principles*. Winter Park, FL: Anna Publishing, Inc., 1977.

Fixx, James F. *The Complete Book of Running*. New York: Random House, 1977.

Foster, Bill. *Conditioning for Basketball: A Guide for Coaches and Athletes*, West Point, N.Y.: Leisure Press, 1980.

Gable, Dan and Peterson, James A. *Conditioning for Wrestling: the Iowa Way.* West Point, N.Y.: Leisure Press, 1980.

Groch, Dick. *Mastering Baseball.* Chicago, IL: Contemporary Books, Inc., 1978.

Jackson, Dennis. *Stretching for Athletics.* West Point, N.Y.: Leisure Press, 1981.

Lydiard, Arthur with Gilmour, Garth. *Running the Lydiard Way.* P.O. Box 366, Mountain View, CA: World Publications, Inc., 1978.

Myers, Clayton R. *The Official YMCA Physical Fitness Handbook.* New York: Popular Library, 1975.

Parker, R.S. *Getting Started in Track and Field: A Coaching Manual.* Los Altos, CA: Tafews, Book Division of Track and Field News, 1976.

Parkhouse, Bonnie L. & Lapin, Jackie. *Women Who Win: Exercising Your Rights in Sports.* Englewood Cliffs, N.J.: Prentice-Hall, Inc., 1980.

Ricci, Benjamin. *Physical and Physiological Conditioning for Men.* Dubuque, IA: Brown Company Publishers, 1966.

Riley, Daniel P. *Strength Training by the Experts.* West Point, N.Y.: Leisure Press, 1982.

Sheehan, George. *Running and Being: the Total Experience.* New York: Simon & Schuster, 1978.

————. *The Encyclopedia of Athletic Medicine.* Mt. View, CA: World Publications, 1972.

Tutko, Thomas and Tosi, Umberto. *Sports Psyching: Playing Your Best Game All of the Time.* Los Angeles, CA: J.P. Tarcher, Inc., 1976.

Valentine, Kim. *Teen-age Distance Running.* Los Altos, CA: Tafnews, Book Division of Track and Field News, 1973.

Vandeweghe, Ernest M. and Flynn, George L. *Growing With Sports: A Parent's Guide to the Young Athlete,* Englewood Cliffs, N.J.: Prentice-Hall Inc., 1979.

# Index

# About the Author

ROBERT GARDNER is chairman of the science department at Salisbury School, Salisbury, Connecticut, where he is also coach of the baseball team. He did his undergraduate work at Wesleyan University and has graduate degrees from Trinity College and Wesleyan. He has taught at a number of National Science Foundation teacher institutes, including one in Ajmer, India.

Mr. Gardner is the author of a number of books for young people, including *Basic Lacrosse Strategy, Kitchen Chemistry, Moving Right Along,* and most recently, *The Whale Watchers' Guide.*